THE KISS OF JESUS

Donna-Marie Cooper O'Boyle

THE KISS OF JESUS

How Mother Teresa and the Saints
Helped Me to Discover the
Beauty of the Cross

IGNATIUS PRESS   SAN FRANCISCO

Cover photos of the author by John Kane
Cover design by Enrique Javier Aguilar Pinto

© 2015 by Ignatius Press, San Francisco
All rights reserved
ISBN 978-1-58617-916-8
Library of Congress Control Number 2014944001
Printed in the United States of America ∞

I lovingly dedicate this book to my children: Justin, Chaldea, Jessica, Joseph, and Mary-Catherine. I also dedicate *The Kiss of Jesus* to my parents, Eugene Joseph Cooper and Alexandra Mary Cooper, and to my brother Gary and my sister Barbara (who have passed on to eternal life). Finally, this book is dedicated to my friends in heaven: Servant of God Father John A. Hardon, S.J., Blessed Mother Teresa of Calcutta, and Saint John Paul II, who blessed my work on Mother Teresa.

CONTENTS

PREFACE

Everyone has a story, unique among all others. All of us, at various times of our lives, share at least a part of ourselves with those who are close to us. Sometimes we might even share some deeply personal matters with complete strangers. Our hearts seek to reach out, after all. Even so, I never planned to write about my own life, to make my personal story an open book for the world. *The Kiss of Jesus* came about after years of writing numerous books about faith and family in an attempt to help those who are traveling the straight and narrow road that leads to eternal life (and hopefully some of those who have yet to begin the journey).

Many years ago when I first began to write, I made sure I kept myself out of the writing as much as I could. I didn't feel a need to draw any attention to myself. Over time, I began to include personal anecdotes—ever so lightly. Eventually I opened up a bit more by sharing bits and pieces of my life with people in need and also in my writings and talks. But one day something happened that dramatically changed my thinking.

After I presented a keynote speech at a women's conference in San Antonio, Texas, a Catholic reporter gave me a ride to Corpus Christi, where I would be giving other talks and signing books. The woman had kindly offered to take me on the two-hour drive so that she could have the chance to talk with me.

During the trip, the gracious driver lamented that she was feeling a bit worn down as a single mother raising her growing son alone. I decided to tell her that I had been a single mother to five children for many years and that I felt that God gave me the grace I needed to get through all of the difficulties and challenges that inevitably come with being a single mother and even to discover much beauty and a lot of joy amid the struggle. As I spoke, she practically swerved off the road! She had had no idea that I would understand her plight. But in that moment, a surprising gift of hope jumped into her heart. She enthusiastically proclaimed that if I could do it, she could too!

After praying and pondering about this experience I realized that God wanted me to share more of myself with others. I decided to open the book of my personal journey—the good and the bad, the crazy, the ugly, the scary, and the redemptive—so that with God's grace I could offer hope, especially to those who are struggling on the sometimes precarious or crooked path that leads to heaven.

I hope and pray you will enjoy this book and that by God's grace it will deeply inspire you to follow God's holy will in your own life.

Our Lady of Hope, please help us all.

Donna-Marie Cooper O'Boyle
October 7, 2013
Feast of Our Lady of the Rosary

I

Searching: The Early Years

I

Cradle Catholic: My Crazy, Blessed Life

If thou art willing to suffer no adversity, how wilt thou be the friend of Christ?

—Thomas à Kempis

What you see is not always what you get. Allow me to explain. I have lived a colorful life dappled with some overwhelming struggles but also brimming with amazing joy. Most people don't know the whole story. They might have seen me on my television shows on EWTN, appearing all put together (I hope!), or they might have heard me on the radio. Others know me by reading my numerous books and articles. Many have told me that they are exceedingly thankful because my message has made a positive difference in their lives.

It is wonderful to know that by God's providence I am helping others; it actually keeps me going—that and God's amazing grace. But there is a lot my readership, listenership, and viewership don't know about me, and I think it's time they know more.

Making My Entrance

My father was sitting on his regular barstool at the local tavern in Stamford, Connecticut, when I came into the world. I'm not sure who was sent to get word to him that his daughter was finally born (almost a month late) and to get him out of the dark watering hole and over to the hospital. Back then fathers didn't participate much in their children's births. Still, I suspect my mother must have felt very alone pushing a ten-pounder out by herself. Yes, I weighed in at ten pounds—right on the button. My mother called me her "Dairy Queen baby" because she indulged in a large vanilla soft-serve ice cream cone as often as possible during her pregnancy. It was the one luxury she would allow herself to ease the challenges and discomforts of pregnancy.

I was born at 11:50 P.M., ten minutes before Thanksgiving Day. So I quickly acquired another nickname that I still haven't lived down— "Butterball"! Siblings (and I have a lot of them) would often tease me, threatening to give me a turkey instead of a birthday present each year.

The hubbub of having a new baby in the home settled down rather quickly in the Cooper household. After all, I was baby number seven and the family was used to lots of commotion and crying. Not quite two years later my baby brother, David, came along to complete the family of ten.

Though families tended to be much larger when I was growing up, my mother still caught a lot of flak for not using birth control or for not getting her tubes tied. Not everyone appreciated her openness to life.

My baptismal day was celebrated with great joy by my many relatives. I was dressed all in white frilly and lacy clothes, swaddled in a white blanket and carried into Saint Mary's church on a brisk December day. I slept entirely through the transforming sacrament; most likely I was content with a full tummy and didn't mind the water being poured over my head and dripping on my face. And so, another Cooper baby was washed clean by Baptism and initiated into the Catholic Church. In my case it was on the last Sunday of Advent, just one week before Christmas—a day of rejoicing in more ways than one. After the church service, the family got together at our house on Lockwood Avenue to carry on their celebration.

My mother had her hands full with lots of children running around the house, mounds of never-ending laundry, dishes multiplying in the kitchen sink, and plenty of clothes to mend. The many rooms with sloping crooked floors needed sweeping, and the shabby furniture needed dusting in our sprawling old house. Now there was another baby to care for, but Mother managed her household with much grace, and with the help of her older children.

Once when I was still a baby an older sibling flung me across the room to protest against minding me while our mother prepared dinner. Fortunately I landed on a bed. Every family has its arguments and growing pains—but we would hope those don't include throwing babies, if I may say so myself!

A typical toddler, I was fascinated with electrical outlets and one day ambled over to investigate one of those funny holes in the wall. I stuck a bobby pin straight in and was immediately shot clear across the room. I have no recollection of flying through the air for a second time. I have been told that my hands were charred black from the sparks that flew out of the outlet. I'm not sure who was supposed to be watching me at the time. No one has owned up to it.

Another time as a toddler I sat on the floor happily playing when I spotted some straight pins, the kind used in sewing. I grabbed them up and put a few in my mouth. One of them poked right through my cheek and out the other side! This I can remember vividly.

A big ruckus ensued as family members ran to me and whisked out the offending pins. My mother then insisted that I eat a lot of bread, presumably to coat any pins I might have swallowed. I survived that ordeal without any further problems (in case you were wondering).

Family Life

I grew up with five brothers and two sisters. My father worked in a factory, and my mother devoted most of her time to raising her children. As we grew she took on various jobs. For a while she cleaned houses. Later when the kids were older she trained to be a home health aide.

My oldest brother, Gene, went to the seminary when I was young, and two other brothers, Gary and Tim, would eventually go off to the Vietnam War. My mother cried and prayed a lot while my brothers were in Vietnam. She added to her own torment for some reason by playing songs about wars and war heroes on her old record player. I could see tears glistening in her eyes every single time. I worried about whether both my brothers would come back alive, and I was exceedingly thankful when they did. But the war took a toll on them as it did on all the troops who witnessed or participated in the violence. Gary, who had been exposed to chemical weapons, died years later from lung cancer.

While Gene studied to be a priest, we were graced with many visits to our home from his fellow seminarians and priests. I always enjoyed their visits, which left me with a peace deep in my soul. I remember one time when Gene, his seminary friend, and I rode bikes down the road singing

"My Favorite Things" from *The Sound of Music*. I balanced my backside on the handlebars of the seminarian's bike and hoped I wouldn't fall off!

My oldest sister, Alice Jean, moved south to Texas, where she met her husband and raised their family. Then Barbara got married too and moved out. I really missed her. I was the only girl left to defend myself from a bunch of active brothers—Tim, Michael, and David. I had to become a tomboy to survive, so I learned to play army with them and to climb trees.

My maternal grandmother visited almost daily. She was a bright spot in my life; it was good to have another female presence besides my mother. She was my only living grandparent and had a sweet way about her, smothering us all with grandmotherly love and making us her famous potato pancakes and Polish cookies and breads.

When not working long hours, my father enjoyed taking his little outboard motorboat onto Long Island Sound. He enjoyed the lull of the waves lapping at the side of the boat while he fished, usually with some of my brothers. We would hear all kinds of fish tales when they came home those evenings, carrying their catch already gutted and wrapped in newspaper.

Father also loved vegetable gardening. He planted a huge garden in our backyard and took great pride in the size and amount of vegetables that came out of his plot of tilled soil. He also took care of many fruit trees—peach, plum, and cherry—that surrounded our backyard paradise.

Pots of homemade spaghetti sauce simmered regularly on our old kitchen stove, pot roasts (the cheaper grades) roasted in the oven, tomatoes were canned, jars and jars of peach jam were carefully preserved, and pies, cakes, and cookies were baked with ample doses of love. Our home always smelled of a rich family life. Though my mother was always busy looking after the eight of us and dealing with all of our antics, she set a warm tone for family dinners, which she promptly served at more or less the same time each evening.

Growing up in the Cooper clan, we always knew when it was Sunday. The day was occupied with attending Mass, going on family outings, and visiting with relatives, either at their homes or ours. We enjoyed a special dinner together in the afternoon, even if pickings were slim. My mother creatively churned out great meals from scratch. At night we gathered again at the table to eat a lighter meal, and then we watched family shows on television while delighting in our ritual Sunday night ice cream.

There were plenty of family weddings to attend and funerals too. At each wedding on my mother's side of the family, at least a few polkas were played and the older folks would dance. Some older women wore colorful Polish dresses. I never learned the polka myself, though I enjoyed watching the dancers hop and spin.

The fashion police might not have approved of my mother's wardrobe, since she was sure to dress her eight children first before thinking of anything new for herself. Her clothes were a bit old, but she always looked pretty to me, especially with the bright red lipstick she put on each time she went out.

Even though we lived in a city, we had a spacious, beautiful backyard. It seemed to stretch for miles, because my little legs took a long while to reach the end. Red roses climbed an arbor and a split-rail fence, which led down to the vegetable and flower gardens in the back. Beautiful weeping willows graced the property too. I spent almost every sunny day playing outside. The great forsythia bushes became castles or huts, depending upon what my imagination decided they should be that day, and I sat beneath the large bowed branches eating juicy, plump red tomatoes I had plucked straight from the garden. For these adventures I came prepared, with a salt shaker in my pocket.

Our backyard served as a wonderful gathering place for our many relatives for all kinds of occasions. For their twenty-fifth wedding anniversary party, my parents rented an enormous tent and set it up in the yard. Their shindig was complete with polka music, of course. I can still see my grandmother making her way through the gathering, snapping shots of the relatives with her trusty Brownie camera, all the while mingling with everyone and bringing smiles to their faces.

She became well known for her photography. "Look at the birdie!" she would say and then snap away. We couldn't count the number of photo albums at her home.

Oftentimes my parents filled an old red wagon with picnic and barbecue foods and we all ventured down to the backyard. It was quite a family parade going through the arbor and down to the old-fashioned barbecue pit. That familiar spot close to the weeping willows was a fine refuge for us—we were living in the city, but were blessed with the charm of the country.

One of my very favorite sights and smells was the hedge of lilac bushes all across our backyard. The fragrance of those beautiful purple and lavender blooms wafted through the air with every spring breeze. Big bouquets of lilacs in vases adorned our home too.

Lucky for me there was a school playground down the street where I used to play with my brothers and a few friends. Most days I took a walk with my grandmother and mother to the corner store, where I became the happy recipient of a couple of pieces of penny candy. Amid the busyness of family life, we also squeezed in regular trips to the park and occasionally the Stamford Museum and Nature Center. Once, while visiting the farm animals there, my cousin Betsy and I secretly unlatched the gate to the donkey pen. We thought he must have been sad to be confined, and we wanted to set him free! I wonder if anyone relatched the gate before he got out.

Along with the blessings of growing up in our large Catholic family there was unavoidable strife. Some arguing is normal, but we children also witnessed some severe fights between our parents. My father was overbearing at times, and my mother was the convenient brunt of his unreasonableness. I started to pray for my father at a young age. Many nights we kids retreated fearfully to our bedrooms for safety.

One night, when I was supposed to be in bed, I peered out my second-floor bedroom window because there had been a fight and I could hear that one of my parents had stormed out the door. My siblings and I huddled near the window and pulled back the curtains to get a glimpse of what was unfolding below. The cold air coming through the old windowpanes seemed to slap me in the face. We glimpsed our mother walking quickly down the sidewalk and pulling her jacket tightly around herself against the cold. This was a troubling sight for a little girl. Was she coming back? After a long time of worrying and wondering, I somehow was able to fall asleep that night. I was very thankful to wake up in the morning and see that my mother was back in the house (she had only taken a walk around the block to calm down) and life would go on as usual.

The Nuns and Heaven

I attended Saint Mary's Catholic School for a period of time. I was very much drawn to the sisters who taught there and who always dressed in full habits. I felt a great deal of peace and comfort whenever I was near them. My grandmother often told me that if I became a nun when I grew up I would go straight to heaven when I died. *How could she know that?* I wondered. Yet I trusted her to know what she was saying, and because she seemed so certain, I kept that holy advice stashed away in my mind. *Maybe I will become a nun later in life,* I mused. For now I would focus on being a little girl.

My mother, grandmother, and the religious sisters planted seeds of goodness in my heart and soul and taught me to make time for prayer. Necessity drew the yearning to pray out of me too. There were times that I knew I had to pray—there was no other way. I followed my heart and got on my knees often, usually by the side of my bed, whenever I needed help. I also prayed regularly to keep up a communication with God. It was a practice that brought me deep comfort. I prayed a lot in the car too, sitting in the back seat while my father was driving, sometimes a bit erratically, worrying that we would get into an accident because he had had too much to drink. At such moments, many Our Fathers and Hail Marys were silently offered up from my little girl's heart and soul. I somehow had the grace to know that I could run to prayer whenever I was scared or in need of any help. I expected results and they were delivered.

Sometimes God enlightened me in prayer, as happened when I was about seven years old and didn't want to get in the car with my mother. I had the sudden thought that we were going to crash, but then dismissed it as silly. Later that day as my mom and I headed out to do some errands, the brakes on our old Pontiac failed and we crashed head-on into a stone wall. We weren't hurt, but we were pretty startled. I told my mother that I had known it was going to happen.

"Why didn't you tell me?" she asked in a flustered voice.

But how do you tell someone about your premonition? You usually don't, especially if you're seven years old.

Sometime after that, as I was kneeling by my bed praying my regular night prayers and asking for help and protection for my family, the phone rang. Just then I somehow knew that my Uncle Bill was dead. My mother got off the phone and shared the sad news that indeed, our uncle had suddenly died.

Looking back, I am grateful to have had a habit of prayer and a sense of the Holy Spirit at a young age. My life would unfold in ways I could not have imagined, and over time I would discover how very much I needed God.

2

Unsuspecting Contemplative:
Seeking God in Nature

If you look for Jesus in everything, you will certainly find Him.

—Thomas à Kempis

My seventh year was a turning point in my life. My father decided to move our family out of the big city and into a quieter country area. He had seen enough of Stamford, but mostly he didn't like the fact that crime had rapidly and insidiously encroached closer and closer to our little safe haven on Lockwood Avenue.

It was the early sixties, and my parents were able to secure a mortgage for a fairly nice contemporary ranch house situated on a couple of acres of land on a dirt road in Ridgefield, Connecticut. Upon moving, my mother arranged for a priest to come and bless our new home. One of the first things my father did was to dig up a huge spread of land at the end of the lawn, around which he erected a wire mesh fence.

As he turned the hard ground, my father unearthed many rusty horseshoes. He mused that they might have been from George Washington's horse, which he imagined trotting down Regan Road. Whose horseshoes they were really didn't matter—this would be his new garden. Bushels and bushels of fresh vegetables would come from that piece of soil for years to come. Though my father suffered from many ailments including gout, which caused swelling in his legs and feet, he still found refuge in his garden and puttered around in it whenever he could.

I acquired both my father's passion for growing vegetables and working in the dirt and my mother's love for beautiful flowers, which she planted throughout the yard. She put her personal touches on the inside of the house too, feathering her new nest with her personal style of shabby chic furniture (before the term came into fashion). Our home was a mishmash of décor, but it was warm and comfortable.

Settling In

When we moved to our new home, my mother attempted to enroll us in the Catholic school in town, but there wasn't any room for me in the second grade. So it was decided that we would attend public schools.

I got off to a good start at Ridgebury Elementary School. My teacher was Miss Darling, and she was just that—very kind and loving. As a somewhat shy new student, I found her gentle care comforting.

I had some trouble seeing the blackboard at school, so my parents took me to an eye doctor. It turned out that I needed eyeglasses. When the glasses were ready, I put them on and suddenly everything around me came into crisp focus. On our ride home, I couldn't take my eyes off the trees we passed. I marveled and asked my parents, "Wow! Everyone can see all of the leaves on the trees?" Prior to that day, the leaves had always appeared blended all together in one big mass.

Our family settled in to our new schedule for school and work. My father now rose at 4:30 each morning to drive an hour's commute to Stamford for work, and my mother took care of the kids and household. Every evening when my father's car pulled into the driveway I ran to get his slippers from beside his bed and greeted him at the door. He would sit in his chair, and I would take off his work shoes and replace them with his comfy slippers. It was our little routine.

My brothers got involved in the Boy Scouts (a few of them achieving Eagle Scout), and I was in the Girl Scouts. Scouting got us out of the house and involved with other kids doing wholesome activities.

Sometimes my mother drew her brood together and we knelt in front of a statue of the Blessed Virgin Mary. Mother lit a candle in a small blue glass votive holder and patiently taught us to pray the Rosary. Though we were never perfectly behaved, my mother did her best with her sometimes-unruly bunch and gave us a wonderful tradition—calling upon Mother Mary. The Rosary has stayed with me throughout my life, showing up at times when I least expected it.

Since we were in the public schools, I started in the second grade faith formation classes through our new parish, also named Saint Mary's, where we met after school once a week. My first class presented my first challenge as the new kid.

"Don't tell her how to do it!" one of the boys remarked.

We had each received a snack to eat before class, and the boys saw me fumbling with my milk carton. I had never opened that kind of carton before, and the mean boys refused to help me. I eventually figured it out by myself.

I felt the sting of newness again on the school playground. A girl about my age taunted me while playing with my tennis ball at recess time. She said it belonged to her. I attempted to show her a distinct marking on it that to me proved it was mine. She didn't care. She simply told me that I wasn't going to get it back. I felt powerless and upset by the unfairness of it—she had stolen my tennis ball.

After school that day I sat alone on the grass by the side of my house, pondering and even praying a bit. It was cold, so I pulled my coat around me and allowed my senses to take in nature—feeling the sun offering me its warmth on my face and watching the weeds nearby bow down in graceful unison under the gentle hand of a breeze. The silence and beauty of nature comforted me.

Nature also brought me joy as I cared for our pets and farm animals. Many times I would nurse sick kittens back to good health. I even sheltered injured mice and birds, keeping them in a shoe box outside and letting them go back to the wild when they were better.

Visits to my grandmother in Stamford were a great comfort to me. Many summer mornings my mother and a couple of us kids would get up early and go to Stamford with my father. He would drop us off at Grandma's house for the day and pick us up when he was ready to go home from work. My grandmother always knew how to make me smile. Her home was like a little church. All sorts of simple sacred art decorated the walls. Her love for the Church was apparent, and her faith was instrumental in igniting the flame of belief in my heart.

Only one thing unsettled me about my grandmother's apartment: the cockroaches. Every time she opened a kitchen cabinet, to get a cup or a dish, dozens of roaches went scurrying in every direction. In her senior citizen apartment building, the roaches came with the apartment and were impossible to eradicate.

Country Life

Our new home was very much in the country, and that brought its own unwanted wildlife. One day when playing in a field across the street from my house, I screamed to my brother.

"Michael!"

A snake had coiled around his leg, its mouth wide open and ready to strike. At the sound of my scream, Michael looked down and shook his leg loose from the snake before it bit him. We quickly ran out of the field. It sure was a close call. We were more careful after that incident not to play in the fields with tall grass where the snakes lived, because some snakes in our area were poisonous.

Now that we were in the country, we thought we might as well get some chickens. So my father built a chicken coop and created a fenced area for them to run and peck in the dirt for bugs. We had several varieties of chickens and a few roosters, who were fierce about protecting their hens. Many a time a brother went into the chicken coop to feed the chickens and a rooster would jump up on his back, hang onto the waistband of his pants, and mercilessly peck at him.

We also acquired a few ducks and rabbits, and even some pheasants. We enjoyed fresh chicken eggs daily and eventually chicken meals (before I realized that we were eating the old hens).

Our trusty and ferocious watchdog Jet (named for his shiny black coat) was a Labrador retriever that patrolled the chicken coop to keep an eye on things. He once took a chomp out of the back of my leg because I was chasing my brothers during a game. I still have an indentation on my leg from the bite.

One day when my grandmother came up from Stamford to visit us at our new house, I could hear some whispering going on among the adults. Then they all congregated by the chicken coop. I'll never forget what happened next. I saw a chicken running around without a head! I was horrified and fascinated all at once. But, that's what happens when you raise chickens for eggs and eating. Eventually their heads get chopped off and they go into the pot for dinner.

The chickens would occasionally escape over the tall fence and walk around our yard searching for worms and bugs to eat. They also ate cat food alongside my cats, right out of their dishes. At one time I had seventeen cats, thanks to a couple of litters. I always talked my parents into allowing me to keep the kittens, since they would grow up and help to keep the mice at bay. Sometimes cats were dropped off at our house too. I imagine people figured that we had so many animals we could certainly take in more.

One summer day when the kittens were playing in the backyard, I went running out to feed them. One of my brothers had previously taken the garbage out and had dropped a few items. He thought he had cleaned them all up. But when I was jogging through the yard, I stepped right on a broken mayonnaise jar that went straight into the center of my foot. I wasn't wearing any shoes (even though my father had told me a million times to wear shoes outside).

At first I didn't realize I had cut my foot, because the broken glass was razor sharp. But a moment later my left foot felt as if it were being squeezed. I lifted it to take a look and discovered it was bleeding profusely. It looked as though a faucet of blood had been turned on in the center of my foot. Suddenly the pain set in, and I felt as if I were going to die. Frightened out of my mind, I quickly hopped up the back porch steps to the door and showed my foot to my mother.

"Look what I just did!"

She met me at the door and was horrified upon seeing the gaping wound and gushing blood. She told me to put my foot up in the nearby bathroom sink, and then thrust my foot under the spout and turned on the cold water full blast, sending frigid water right into the open hole in my foot. The gash was about four inches long and went down to the bone. My father came around the corner and saw us in the bathroom.

"Jesus Christ!" he blurted out. He turned as white as chalk and had to sit down. At least he called upon Jesus! Someone phoned for the ambulance while my mother handed me a thick towel and helped me wrap it around my foot. She helped me to hobble over to the couch in the living room, where I elevated my throbbing foot on a few pillows. I had recently taken a first aid course with the Girl Scouts and knew I had to keep it elevated.

The ambulance driver arrived and slowly opened the blood-soaked towel to check the wound. Upon seeing it, his hands began to tremble. I mean they really shook, and so did my confidence in the man's abilities. He placed some gauze pads over the wound and rewrapped the towel.

My mother rode in the back of the ambulance with me. She knew it was serious. I kept saying, "They better give me some kind of pain reliever before they stitch it—they will, won't they?" Mom assured me that the hospital doctor would take care of that.

Well, he sure did. I received a few injections of novocaine right into the center of the wound—ouch! My foot was then stitched up on the inside and the outside. I then needed time to heal.

Horse Fever

Before long I came down with horse fever, a condition common to pre-teen and teenage girls. I wanted a horse so badly and I wanted to learn to ride—I was horse crazy. I joined the 4-H club in my area and learned about the care and handling of horses and then horseback riding.

Once at a riding lesson the horse in front of me bucked at my horse, and kicked me in the shin instead. One of the most excruciating pains I ever felt was when those iron horseshoes struck my leg with brute force. I had to get off my horse and have my leg checked. After determining that my leg was probably not broken, the riding instructor made me get back on my horse. I obeyed with wobbly and shaking legs.

Getting hurt was one of the risks of horseback riding—not being able to read the mind of the animal you are sitting on means you never know what might happen. Indeed, horses have minds of their own, and humans cannot always contain or control them. It's not like driving a race car that you can stop whenever you want to. Horses are living beings that can get scared and react by running or bucking. Still, I loved horses and everything about them. I relished every ride, especially cantering through open fields with the wind in my face and natural beauty all around me.

Any time I could, I would go downtown to Young's feed store, where I would practically drool over the horse tack and dream of one day owning my own horse. The smells of the leather tack and horse paraphernalia got me high. I bought a lead rope so that I could dream about leading my horse with it one day. I told you, I was crazy—horse crazy! But I wasn't alone in this regard. I knew other girls who felt the same way. When I wasn't reading Nancy Drew mysteries, my nose was inserted in every horse book I could find from the library. I passionately desired to know everything about horses, including how to build the barn. I even pored over the want ads looking for horses for sale.

I did a lot of babysitting for families in my area of Ridgefield. I was actually in demand. I loved kids, and they seemed to enjoy my company too. Every dollar I received for caring for children (and I garnered a whole dollar per hour) was stashed away for "someday"; someday I was going to buy a horse. I shared my aspirations with my parents, who either didn't think I was serious or just hoped I would lose interest after a while. After all, they had eight kids and constant worries about paying the bills and keeping a roof over our heads. They couldn't waste time worrying about their daughter getting a horse. But I wasn't going to lose interest—I was determinedly horse crazy.

One day I convinced my parents to take me to look at horses. It just worked out that they were both in a good mood and the farm was only a couple of towns away. I fell instantly in love with a beautiful bay. My brother Michael suddenly became interested in horses too. So we ended up buying two horses on some sort of payment plan. They would be delivered in a few weeks or so after we had time to erect a simple stable and put up some fencing. My dream was coming true!

The momentous day arrived. I watched intently from the living room window for the truck and horse trailer to arrive. It finally drove up our long driveway and stopped at the top. The two horses were carefully backed out of the trailer. A couple of saddles and bridles were taken out too. None too originally, I named my horse Star because of the large white mark on his forehead. My brother named his white gelding Blue Boy for his big blue eyes.

I enjoyed every bit of time I spent with Star—riding and grooming him, even cleaning out his stall. Michael and I rode our horses all over our property and down our dirt road. But I grew concerned for Star, who was looking a bit thin and coughed and wheezed every now and again. I wasn't an expert on horses but I knew I had to keep an eye on his health.

Within two weeks after Star arrived, he suddenly dropped to the ground. He was dead! I was in disbelief and cried very hard. The veterinarian explained that he died from "shipping fever". In other words, the horse must have been very sick when we got him. The seller had disguised Star's illness and had taken advantage of us green-behind-the-ears novices. We all took turns with shovels, digging Star's grave. When it was deep enough, we dragged him to the hole and covered him with dirt mixed with my tears. It seemed so unfair that I had to bury my own horse.

We complained vehemently to the seller and ended up giving back Blue Boy to get out of the payment plan. We heard that it wasn't the first time this kind of thing happened to unsuspecting folks because of this guy's dishonesty. It made me angry that someone would do something corrupt like this to trick a child. We learned a hard lesson.

Again, I sought refuge and time alone with God, sitting in a quiet place outside—just pondering and listening.

Along Came Sundran

As time went by, our hearts healed from the sadness of losing our horses, and a couple of years later I began to look at horse ads again. One day I found an interesting ad and begged my parents to take me to see the horse. There was something about the sound of this horse that was intriguing, and the price was right too. And I had been saving up my babysitting money. My parents agreed and we set out for the farm.

When we arrived, a strawberry roan Tennessee Walker came trotting toward the gate from across the field. He seemed to be whinnying to me. He was beautiful! The owner remarked that his horse Sundran must have thought I was his niece Barbara, of whom the horse was very fond. He said I even looked like her. Sundran took to me and I to him immediately. It certainly seemed like it was a match that was meant to be. The man was delighted to think that his horse could be cared for by someone resembling his niece both in mannerisms and appearance. Since he was also getting on in years and no longer able to care for the horse, he sold Sundran to us at a ridiculously low price, and I couldn't have been happier.

My father, my brothers, and I built a one-stall barn and got the corral ready for Sundran. I couldn't wait for the day he would be delivered to us. Sundran was very bright and healthy, and even knew how to do some playful tricks. He could open up a mailbox, stamp his hooves to count, and stretch out his legs to get lower to the ground, making him easier to mount.

On the second day Sundran was with us, as I was cantering bareback up a hill in our yard, I accidentally dropped my rein. As I tried to reach it, I fell off the horse. My left arm hurt intensely, but I downplayed it so that my parents wouldn't be upset.

My arm throbbed all night long. By morning my wrist was swollen and still very painful. A trip to the hospital for X-rays was in order, and they revealed a fracture of the wrist. It was a bit of a setback and a huge disappointment, since I had just gotten my horse and now couldn't ride him for a while.

After my arm healed I had lots of fun with Sundran, riding around my yard and the dirt roads near my house, competing in horse shows, and taking part in parades. I spent hours polishing my tack, grooming my horse, and braiding his mane and tail before each horse show. Once I rode Sundran to high school on Earth Day. In the summer months I rode him a few miles to a nearby horse farm to swim with him in the lake. A few of my horse-lover friends and I rode our horses bareback through the refreshing lake. It was absolutely exhilarating. We wrapped parts of our horses' manes around our fingers so we'd have something secure to hang on to when going through the deeper water. Our horses' backs became very slippery; even when we gripped tight with our bare legs, we could easily slide right off if we weren't careful. I loved every minute of it. As our horses exited the other side of the lake, they shook themselves with great gusto, and we again hung on for dear life!

Because we raised chickens on our mini-farm, some neighboring families wanted to buy our fresh eggs. For the absurdly low price of fifty cents a dozen, I delivered the eggs to the customers on horseback. I rode Sundran a few miles bareback with the egg cartons under my arm, a couple of dozen at a time. It was always a pleasant outing.

3

Thrift Shop Girl: Getting By with Secondhand Clothes

> Therefore do not be anxious about tomorrow, for tomorrow will be anxious for itself. Let the day's own trouble be sufficient for the day.
>
> —Gospel of Matthew

My elementary school years went well for the most part. One time my teacher asked us to raise our hands when she called out the number of children in our families. She started counting. She never did get to number eight, and I was too shy to raise my hand to let her know.

My fourth grade teacher, Mr. Wilkes, was very impressed with a booklet I made for a writing assignment. He unintentionally but thoroughly embarrassed me in front of the class by holding it up and practically gushing over it, pointing out the fine word structure and the expressive illustrations. I wanted to sink down in my seat and hide under my desk. I'm sure my face turned many shades of red.

Later on in sixth grade I was again embarrassed in front of my classmates. My teacher called on me and made some sort of peculiar remark about me liking a boy and looking at him instead of looking at the board. It was an attempt at humor, but it caught me totally off guard. I couldn't have been more mortified. Being so sensitive, I burst into tears.

I was very interested in art and loved every art class—whether it was ceramics, drawing, or painting. I was in the chorus and also took up playing the violin. My father, my older brother Gene, and my sister Alice Jean all played the violin. I felt drawn to it. After a couple of years of study, I joined the school orchestra and played at the school concerts. At some point I missed a couple of lessons due to sickness, and when

I went back to orchestra class the teacher said, "Look what the wind blew in!" There was something about her tone that bothered me, and I never went back after that. I suddenly lost interest in playing the violin for fear of being ridiculed. I can kick myself now because I wish I had continued.

School Fashion and Thrift Shop Clothes

There was a lot of wealth in our town, and school sometimes felt more like a fashion show than a place for learning. I wore plain clothes, nothing special compared to the everyday finery of some of my classmates. I began to feel that I didn't quite fit in. Yet there was not much I could do about it. I didn't want to bug my parents for new clothes because I knew they were doing their best to provide for us.

Once in a while we went to the local department store for a new pair of jeans, a blouse, or a pair of shoes, but most of the time my mom shopped for us at the local thrift shop. I was mortified at the thought of being seen there, or of an article I was wearing being recognized by its former owner. I was constantly looking over my shoulder every time my mother took me there. I did find some interesting items. I picked up a pair of used riding boots for a good price, and I found some appealing horse books. But I certainly didn't want anyone from school to know that we shopped there. I would have been incredibly embarrassed, and my social life at school would probably have been a lot more challenging if my classmates had found out.

I smile as I write these words about my abhorrence of secondhand stores, because all of my children absolutely love shopping at thrift and consignment shops. Now, it's actually a fashionable thing to do!

Despite our family income differences, I managed to get along with my classmates. The cliques of girls intimidated me, so I stuck mainly with my few close friends and tried not to let the popular girls get to me.

In addition to one's clothes, one's hairstyle had to be just right. One time a girl got up out of her seat and walked over to me before the teacher came into the classroom. She didn't say a word as she plucked my hair out from behind my ear. She then said I shouldn't wear my hair that way since I had it pulled back on top. Maybe she was trying to help me, but most probably she wanted to demonstrate her place in the pecking order by dictating to me how I should look to please her and others.

Fashions changed quickly at school, and it was hard to keep up with them. All of a sudden saddle shoes made a comeback, and the popular girls started wearing them. My friend Kathy and I eventually broke down and bought some. For the most part though, we had our own styles and tried not to pay a lot of attention to the cliques.

The cliques seemed to pay attention to us, though. One time Kathy and I decided to try to start a little trend. We went to the army and navy surplus store and purchased some men's khaki work pants and began to wear them to school. Very soon after we noticed the popular girls wearing the same kind of pants!

Kicked to the Curb

In junior high school Betty (not her real name) moved to Ridgefield from another state. She sat next to me in one of our classes, in the back on the right side of the room. Betty was pretty, had long blond hair, and was kind. We became fast friends and spent time together until one day she dropped me. Without warning she kicked me to the curb. Perhaps because she had become one of the popular girls, she no longer had time to talk to me.

One day as I was racing to class, something hit me in the chest and landed on top of the pile of books in my arms. I glanced down to discover what appeared to be a folded-up note. *What the heck?*

I quickly grabbed it, stuffed it into my purse, and kept making my way through the mob of students toward my class. I had a study hall after this class, and I thought I would read the note at that time. Of course the class dragged on as if it would never end, and when the bell finally rang I shot out of my seat and scurried to study hall as quickly as possible. Sliding into my seat in the assembly hall, I pulled out the bulky, folded triangular note and read it.

"Dear Woodchuck," it began. "We call you Woodchuck because of your teeth." Instantly tears brimmed in my eyes, but I continued reading the degrading and mean-spirited letter. Worst of all, it was signed by three of my so-called friends! I was shocked and devastated. The bell would ring again in about half an hour, and I would go home. *It can't happen soon enough*, I thought. I hoped I wouldn't see any of those three friends. I didn't want anyone to see my red eyes, either. After that last period I made a dash for my locker and then the bus.

I couldn't tell anyone about it at home. I just kept wondering how my three friends could have done that to me. How mean girls at that age can be to each other!

Somehow I made it through the next day at school and the days that followed. Whenever I saw my former friends, I acted as though nothing had happened. I didn't want to reveal my vulnerable and pummeled heart, nor did I want to hold anything against them. Life would have to go on, but in a different way.

I took great delight in getting home from school each day and running up to the barn to see my horse. I brought him carrots, which he ate right up. I caressed his face and scratched behind his ears and talked to him. He talked to me too—he whinnied to me and nuzzled my face with his wet mouth slobbering on me. I didn't care about getting messy from horse kisses. I just wiped it off. I put Sundran's bridle on him, jumped up and swung my leg over his back. I gave him a quick squeeze with my legs and we took off for a ride. Each time one of his hoofs hit the ground, another bit of frustration and sadness went through me and into him and was then pounded into the ground—nothing magical, that's just what happens when you ride a horse and you are one with him and with nature. I was one with God most especially, and I could pray as I rode.

Another Jolt

There were school dances, crushes on boys, track and field, extracurricular activities, clubs, good causes, tons of homework, and plenty of things to hold my attention during the junior high and high school years.

I hung out with my true friends, and we did our best to navigate the challenging years of growing up, striving to make some kind of difference in our own little part of the world in our distinctive ways, and trying to have fun too. Just when things were starting to settle down a little, life threw me another jolt.

Each summer my family and friends would go to the Great Danbury Fair, a hundred-year-old agricultural fair and carnival for local folks and crowds of visitors from all over. For nine days acres of land were filled with amusement rides, animals, games, art exhibits, attractions, contests, cotton candy, hot dogs, hot apple pie, and all the other delights of a country fair that children and families love. I enjoyed the agricultural part of the huge fair as much as I liked the scary rides and carnival games. People in our area took full advantage of the fair, going as many days as possible.

One experience at the fair stands out very clearly in my mind. I saw a young boy, about six or seven years old, walking around the fair all alone and nervously chewing on the tattered cuffs of his long-sleeved sweatshirt. I realized he must be the son of a carnival worker and probably did a lot of traveling as the fair moved from place to place across the country. It broke my heart to see him. Clearly no one was keeping an eye on him, and I was concerned. When the boy saw me watching him he quickly scurried away to a man who looked to be his father. Seeing that boy touched my heart in a profound way, implanting in me a deep desire to help others.

When I was fifteen years old, I had a more harrowing experience at the Danbury Fair. While enjoying the rides and games of chance, I started conversing with a guy who ran one of the game booths. He seemed interested in talking with me, and I didn't mind. What teenage girl would mind a cute guy taking an interest in her? I went home later that day feeling rather contented.

The following day I went to the fair again and went on my favorite rides, ate some fried dough, and hung around the same young man I had met at the games the day before. He told me that he had a break coming up and was going to walk to his trailer to get a pain reliever for his headache, and he invited me to come along. I was excited to be asked. Naïve about certain kinds of men, I had no idea what he might be expecting. So, when his break time came around I walked with him to his trailer located in a back parking lot, a long distance from the carnival festivities. He invited me up the few steps into the trailer, and as soon as I was inside he quickly closed the door and locked it, putting the key in his pocket. Whatever air was in that dingy trailer seemed to vanish.

Then the unspeakable happened.

He unzipped his pants, lay back on the threadbare, unmade bed and told me what I had to do while threatening that he wouldn't let me out of the trailer until I did it. I almost died of revulsion and fright.

A short while later I bolted out of the trailer as soon as he opened the door, and I ran as fast as my legs would take me until I couldn't breathe. Then I stopped, caught my breath, and ran some more. Eventually, I made it to the place where I was to meet my ride home and just waited there. I don't know how long I was there. I didn't care.

I couldn't say a word to anyone about what had happened. It would be years before I would disclose it. Remarkably, about thirty-five years later something incredible would occur at that very place.

Jesus Freak

During my teen years I got involved with parish youth retreats that gave me occasional time away to think and to pray. I did a lot of meditating and soul searching during the retreats and some writing as well.

Once on retreat, I was praying and pondering and watching a little bird with great interest. As I observed the bird flying back and forth I asked myself, *Am I like that bird flying aimlessly from place to place?* Although I know now that birds don't fly about without cause, at the time the bird seemed to lack direction. *Do I have direction?* I wondered. *What does God want from me and for me?* Wanting to follow God's holy will for my life, I reflected upon what it could be.

I think these retreat experiences helped to keep my teenage emotions steady in order to grow closer to God. Because I professed my belief in God, I was made fun of by some students at school who called me a "Jesus freak". I didn't go around preaching or carrying a Bible. I did wear a cross (which would grow to be an integral part of my life), and being sensitive made me an easy target for teasing.

I took driving lessons, got my license, and eventually bought a cheap old jalopy. It was a push-button Plymouth Valiant. I actually pushed buttons to change the gears on the car!

I got my first job stocking shelves at a new drug store, and I learned cashiering too. I moved on to working at a grocery store and stayed employed there for a few years, moving up to the position of the bakery department manager.

One of the things I had to do as the bakery manager was to discard perfectly good baked goods when they expired. This deeply bothered me even at sixteen years of age. I secretly spread the word when I would be throwing away food, and at those times people in need would congregate outside at the back of the store, where I would give them the outdated items instead of throwing them into the dumpster. My mother was there on occasion too. I could have lost my job if I had gotten caught, but that was a risk I was willing to take in order to help hungry people.

In our spare time, my friend Kerry (not her real name) and I began to attend a Bible study for youth, which was facilitated by a Catholic priest in a neighboring town. Kerry and I worked together at the grocery store, and we made many new friends, learned more about our faith, and stayed out of trouble by hanging out with Christians—a good thing for teenagers to do.

I started dating a guy named Matthew (not his real name), whom I met among the friends I socialized with at the Bible study meetings. He was a bit older than I and an ex-Marine who had served in Vietnam. We enjoyed one another's company and went to my senior prom together.

One day on our way to work, my friend Kerry and I observed a few members of Hare Krishna, also known as the International Society for Krishna Consciousness, a group connected with Hinduism. As they wandered around the parking lot in their saffron robes, panhandling and peddling their wares, we saw one of our friends giving them some money and in return receiving a book. Kerry and I quickly put our heads together and decided we should give our friend some money and ask for the book so that we could throw it away. We wanted to protect him. We felt that the book would contaminate his mind and possibly draw him into the weird beliefs of the Krishnas. We were praying that he would turn to Christianity instead. So we handed our friend six dollars, the exact amount he paid for the book, and we told him he could buy beer with it if he wanted to and we would take the book off his hands. He gladly made the exchange, and Kerry and I happily tore the book up and threw its ripped pages into the trashcan outside the grocery store.

Seemingly out of nowhere two Hare Krishnas appeared and viciously lunged at us. Only minutes before, they had been all the way on the other side of the parking lot. Without warning, one of them slammed me on the side of my head with a huge book he had grabbed out of the cloth bag hanging on his shoulder.

He screamed in my face, "That's offensive! That's offensive!", and each time walloped my head with the book. The other guy grabbed hold of Kerry's shoulders and pinned her against the grocery store window. It was unbelievable. Nearby shop owners came running out of their stores, but nobody helped us. Perhaps the fact that people were at least taking notice finally sent the Krishnas sprinting for their van, never to be seen again.

As soon as I was freed from the head pounding, I rushed over to the pay phone right outside the store and struggled to put a nickel in the coin slot. My hand was trembling and I felt stunned from the pain in my head. The phone call wouldn't go through—just as in a nightmare when you can't get help and nothing seems to work right. It took a few seconds for me to remember that I had to find another nickel in my purse or pocket to be able to make my phone call because at that time pay phones required ten cents. I found the nickel and called the police.

The police arrived shortly thereafter, and Kerry and I were taken in the squad car to the station, where we answered several questions and gave our formal complaints. That was it. As far as we know, the disgruntled Hare Krishnas were never caught or held responsible for assaulting us.

Graduating

Back at school, I filled my schedule with as many art classes as possible and also signed up for journalism class, which I enjoyed. I began writing pieces for the school newspaper.

Gone were the days of the comfortable old high school with all its charm and character—from its crooked, sloping halls to its graffiti-decorated bathrooms—because a new high school had opened in another area of town, and my class would be the first to graduate from there. Most students likened the new school architecture to that of a prison, but we would be there only one year.

With high school graduation fast approaching, I kept busy completing assignments and taking part in the activities of each day. Some days were pretty good, others made me wish I could hurry up and get my diploma and get out of there. Truthfully most of them fell into the latter category.

The June evening arrived, and I donned my white cap and gown and processed to receive my diploma. A chapter in my life had closed, and a new, much more challenging one was about to begin.

II

Survival: Begging For Mercy

4

Kidnapped: Pleading with God

More than that, we rejoice in our sufferings, knowing that suffering produces endurance, and endurance produces character, and character produces hope, and hope does not disappoint us, because God's love has been poured into our hearts through the Holy Spirit who has been given to us.

—Letter of Paul to the Romans

After high school I had no inclination to go to college. My high school guidance counselors didn't encourage me to go to college. More importantly, my parents didn't encourage me to further my education. They were living paycheck to paycheck and didn't have the funds to pay for it. I continued to work at the grocery store and to attend the Bible study meetings in the neighboring town. I was still dating Matthew.

One day, seemingly out of the blue, Matthew handed me an engagement ring and asked me to marry him, and I said yes. I was young and naïve. Months later, while drying my hands in the bathroom at Matthew's parents' home, I accidentally banged my left hand on the wall. The diamond in my engagement ring cracked. I thought diamonds were supposed to be extremely strong, and I was very upset that I had wrecked my ring. I found out, however, that it was a fake diamond; that didn't bother me as much as finding out that it was a used ring too. Matthew had bought it from a friend whose engagement had ended. Still, like pretty much everything else, I accepted it without complaining. I wore my cracked used ring.

After a while I decided it was time to move out of my parents' home. I began scouting out affordable apartments, poring over the want ads, and asking friends and acquaintances. A young woman I worked with told me about an available room for rent in her apartment in the same town where I attended the Bible study. Two other young women rented rooms there as well.

My mother was not happy with my decision to move out, but I was not happy at home. I needed to move out for my own sanity. I loved my parents, but the strife in the house weighed heavily on me; I felt trapped and suffocated. Since I couldn't fix the situation at home, moving seemed like a good option.

Moving day was emotional, to say the least. Mom cried. I think I broke her heart. I moved into the room at my friend's apartment in a neighboring town and commuted to work each day.

Matthew visited me at my apartment, and I visited him at his. I started spending a lot of time at Matthew's since there was always a lot of commotion at my new place. I stayed overnight one time when it got late and I was too tired to drive back to my apartment. After a while, for the sake of convenience, I moved into Matthew's apartment. I trusted Matthew, who offered me a separate room, so I did not see at the time that living with him would place me in a compromising situation. Having gotten used to my new environment and not caring for the commute to Ridgefield every day, I eventually quit my job, figuring I would get another one closer to my new area. I was too young and inexperienced to see where my reliance on Matthew could lead.

I can't put my finger on exactly when it was that things started to change, but change they did. Matthew stopped going to the Bible study and meeting with our friends. Many unfamiliar people were beginning to beat a path to our door. Some days there were about twenty visitors who came and went. Each time the doorbell rang Matthew would rush down the stairs to let them just inside the front door and out of the open. They would exchange a few words and Matthew would come back up to the apartment. He was dealing drugs, I eventually discovered, mostly pot. He told me he needed the money to pay the rent. Even though the landlords lived below us in the first-floor apartment, they didn't seem to suspect anything wrong was going on. I sensed danger but did not know what to do besides moving out as soon as possible. But before I could, something happened.

I don't think I was ever so shocked as the day Matthew pulled out some rifles he had secretly stashed away in the closet. This was the man who previously carried a Bible wherever he went. He seemed calm (too calm, which was eerie) as he spoke to me about them. He said we would need them. I couldn't imagine where they came from or even how long they had been there. As I cautiously questioned him about the need for guns and where he acquired them, his body tensed and his facial expression immediately changed into something unfamiliar to me. Filled with dread, I dropped the subject.

Soon afterward, without warning, Matthew grabbed me and pushed me back, pressing my shoulders against the wall near the front door.

"This is where you will stand," he told me. Then he picked up a rifle.

"You hold it like this," he instructed, shoving it into my arms. "You aim like this and then you blow their heads off when they try to come in!" And he laughed.

I knew for certain that Matthew was unstable and that I had to act as calmly as I could while he was doing all of this. His behavior had become increasingly odd, but this was the first time I saw this side of him. *He is quite capable of murdering me*, I thought, and the realization terrified me. Not until years later did I realize he had suffered some kind of nervous breakdown, perhaps because of his experiences in Vietnam, which contributed to the sudden and extreme changes in his personality.

One day as it was starting to get dark, he told me, "Get in the car. We are going for a ride." He told me that he had to check something out. I had no idea where we were headed, and I was too afraid to ask.

About forty-five minutes later he pulled up in front of my parents' home in Ridgefield. He took the handgun out of the glove compartment and placed it into his pocket and told me to stay in the car. He crept stealthily up the long driveway and circled around to the back of the house in complete darkness. This sneaking around totally undetected was a skill he had learned in the Marines and had used often in Vietnam. My family's ferocious watchdog Jet didn't bark at all. He never even woke up! As I sat in the car trembling, I prayed.

When Matthew returned he let me know in unambiguous terms that he would kill my whole family and me if I didn't do what he said and remain loyal to him. I was no longer a fiancé eagerly awaiting her wedding day, but a captive being held against her will.

Living a Lie

"Get down on the floor," Matthew instructed me.

It was early evening and we had driven to an out-of-town location in his friend's van. I needed to stay out of sight as he and Tommy (not his real name) approached a building. I wasn't sure what was happening, whether it was a drug deal or something else. About fifteen to twenty minutes later, the door of the van slid open where I was hiding. The guys were carrying large duffle bags, which they quickly dumped into the back of the van.

"Let's get outta here," Matthew said, and Tommy sped off.

We got back to Matthew's apartment, and the guys quickly carried the duffle bags into the apartment in the dark. Once inside with the door locked, Matthew and Tommy rifled through the stuff inside the bags. It was a bunch of letters; I think they had robbed a post office. As they ripped open the envelopes they found various amounts of cash, some of it maybe birthday money meant for grandchildren somewhere.

I lived in fear—a fear so deep I couldn't understand its depth. Yet, at times I wasn't even aware of it. Operating in survival mode, I carefully measured my words and actions. I had to pretend to myself that he didn't scare me, believing all the while that I couldn't call for help or my family would be murdered. I also had to convince him that I cared about him, while I secretly planned my escape. My family thought I was merely living with Matthew. They wanted me out of there and tried several times to persuade me to come back home. Once my mother even sent my brother to beg me to leave with him. I couldn't. I was afraid of what might happen.

One of the rare times I was allowed to leave the apartment was to see Mom for Mother's Day, but I couldn't say anything to anyone about what was really going on. Matthew dropped me off at my parents' house, and I had to pretend that I was doing perfectly fine. Matthew must have thought that he had to give me at least some slack or else my family would suspect his evil doings and do something about it. He told me to be ready when he came back for me at five o'clock.

Months passed but I don't recall ever having a calendar. Life was monotonous and terrifying all at once. Days were sometimes never-ending. Many times I just peered out of the second-floor windows. Looking out as far as I could stretch my gaze would sometimes bring me out of my captivity at least a little. And once in a while seeing someone on the street below seemed to help too.

Drugs were sold and wild parties were thrown at the apartment. I stayed to myself whenever I could. Matthew and his friends smoked pot in front of me and many times made a big flaming ball of pot and blew the smoke toward my face while I tried to dodge the clouds, Matthew laughing all the while. It was a very sick sort of laughing. My life was sick, come to think of it.

As I struggled to survive, a part of me was seeking some kind of normalcy amid the craziness. Perhaps I had learned a few of these sorts of coping skills as a child. I might also have been suffering from a phenomenon that has been called Stockholm Syndrome, a condition not studied or named until the early 1970s. In plain language, the syndrome is a psychological response in which a victim becomes bonded or loyal to someone who is terrorizing him. This form of traumatic bonding is named after an incident in which bank robbers held customers and employees in a Swedish bank for more than six days. Upon their release, the victims defended and even tried to help the bank robbers. Some experts believe that this occurred because the criminals showed some signs of kindness and because the victims needed defense mechanisms to protect themselves. This pattern has been observed in other victimizing situations.

Living in captivity and fear draws out an innate instinct to survive. The victim gives priority to perceived life-and-death issues and all others, even safety and personal comfort, take a back seat. A person's ability to think and to act rationally and objectively becomes dramatically impaired. Call it Stockholm Syndrome or survival tactics, only God knows what was going on within me as I lived that hellish life.

One sunny, brisk fall day Matthew decided that we should take a road trip. We got in the car and headed north. It was the same push-button Plymouth Valiant I bought as my first car. It almost seemed bearable sitting in the passenger seat. The sun was bright and streaming in the windows, warming my arms. I felt almost normal.

As the traffic thickened and began clogging the highway, Matthew reached in front of me while he was driving at about 70 miles per hour, opened the glove compartment, and pulled out a loaded handgun. He had a crazed look about him and was clearly becoming enraged about the traffic. He set the gun next to him on his seat, and I was afraid he would kill someone. I silently prayed.

We made it to Vermont in one piece, and I was thankful no one was killed on the way. We checked into a fleabag motel, had something to eat, and went to bed. The next day we stayed a short time in the area before we headed back to Connecticut.

Another Kidnapping

At some point while I was living with Matthew one of my relatives was planning a move to Texas. My mother suggested that I help her with her small children on the plane. Thinking it would be a nice thing to do, I told Matthew about it and he agreed reluctantly that I could go and help as long as I was back right away. Though I was pretty much cut off from the family aside from occasional phone calls, Matthew knew he had to give me some contact with them.

I made the trip to Texas, where my relative would stay temporarily with another relative's family. Shortly after arriving that evening, the relative whose home we were visiting, Charlene (not her real name), took my purse from me. I panicked and asked what she was doing. She said I was not going back to Connecticut.

It was all a setup and had been planned in advance to get me away from Matthew. I was being held against my will. They thought they could "deprogram" me. They were keeping my purse, which held my money and my plane ticket back to Connecticut. I felt sure that Matthew would kill us all.

I screamed something crass I had learned from my dear old dad. I don't think I had ever said it before that moment. It just came out of me when I was feeling so out of control. I soon realized that all I could do was try to calm down and to fake cooperation. I secretly planned an escape in my head and went to bed when everyone else did. I knew that Charlene and her husband would be leaving for work early in the morning. I would have to make a run for it after that and hope the others would sleep in.

I hardly slept at all that night. After Charlene and her husband left, I went into high gear but very quietly. I got dressed and scouted around for my purse. I found it, grabbed my suitcase, and crept out the front door while the others in the house were still sleeping. I had no idea how I would get to the airport, which was over an hour's ride away. I didn't even know which way to go. I started to drag my suitcase (there were no handy wheels on suitcases back then) while making my way as quickly as I could through a field of high grass.

I sensed that someone was following me, and when I turned around I saw it was one of Charlene's older sons. I speeded up, frightened at what would happen to me if I were caught. The field seemed endless, but I finally came upon a busy street on the other side. Not knowing where I was, I glanced all around and spotted a gas station with a police car parked nearby. I managed to drag my bag across the street and over to the squad car. I explained that I had been held against my will by relatives and wanted to get to the airport to go home to Connecticut. I showed him my plane ticket and my driver's license. Since I was about nineteen years old (and legally old enough to be on my own), he drove me to the bus station and told me there would be a bus to the airport.

As I was checking into the prices and schedules at the bus station I bumped into a bus driver who was getting off his shift. When I realized I didn't have enough money for the bus fare, I told him my story, and I think he felt sorry for me. He said he would drive me in his own car all the way to the airport. I was very thankful because I didn't have enough money for the bus fare. I was taking a big chance allowing a stranger to drive me such a distance, but I did it anyway. I figured he was probably safe since he was a bus driver. I was desperate.

When we arrived at the airport the man said to me that he wished we had some time to "get it on". He thought I had to hurry to catch my flight. Thank God he didn't try anything. I quickly exited his car, thanking him for the ride while handing him some cash for gas.

In reality I had to sneak around the airport all day because my flight wasn't until early evening. I hid in several ladies' rooms throughout the day, fearing that Charlene or her family would come to get me.

I made it to Kennedy Airport in New York. Matthew was standing there when I got off the plane. I didn't tell him about being held against my wishes. I feared he would blow a gasket and seek revenge.

Interior Anguish, Pain, and Loss

The apartment reeked of stale coffee grounds, cigarette smoke, and the stubs of burnt joints.

I don't know exactly how many seasons passed while I was there with Matthew. Each morning I woke up and acutely realized that I was still there at the apartment. It wasn't a dream or even an awful nightmare. It was real—my crazy, mixed-up life.

I was getting more and more upset about a couple of Matthew's friends who bragged about blowing pot smoke over their baby's crib and did other irresponsible things. I couldn't stand the guns, the drugs, the drinking, and the sheer lack of anything that seemed to be safe and normal.

The winter was bitter cold and depressing. The snow that outlined the street was dirty and slushy. Each day I plunged deeper into an abyss. Sometimes I couldn't feel anything. Yet, my soul longed for spring—a rebirth—a dose of hope that could come to my heart somehow. I don't know how long it had been since I had gone to Mass. I had to force myself to get through this winter with my sanity intact.

The next weapon in Matthew's arsenal was a semiautomatic machine gun. He seemed very pleased with his new gun. It scared me to death. Even though I was sucked into the crazy world hidden behind the door of that apartment, I still deeply yearned to break free. Somewhere deep within me I hung on to the whisper of a hope that I would eventually make my escape. For now, I had to make it through each day.

Then one morning I shot up in bed with an excruciating jolt of pain. It felt as though a knife had stabbed me in the gut. I got out of bed and was immediately bent over from another blow of intense pain. Blood came gushing down from between my legs. The pains kept coming, and I thought I would scream in agony. But I remained silent in my shock. I was having a miscarriage. I went to the bed and shook Matthew to awaken him. He murmured faintly that he was sleeping.

"Get up quickly; you need to take me to the hospital!" I pleaded.

"Make me a cup of coffee," he demanded.

I went to the kitchen and turned on the stove to boil water. I walked toward the bathroom to see what I could do about the bleeding and crumpled over in pain a couple times on the way. The bleeding was fierce, and I was feeling extremely weak. I realized I had better call a doctor. I called the office and was told that the doctor would meet me at the emergency room and that I should get to the hospital right away.

I hung up the phone. The water was ready. I poured it into the tall white mug with the Union Jack on the side, added instant coffee, sugar, and milk, and gave it a quick stir. I carried the hot coffee to Matthew's bedside, spilling a little trail of it on the way as I inadvertently wiggled the mug with each wince of pain.

"Here's your coffee. Please get up. I have to go to the hospital."

There was no movement from Matthew, who looked like a corpse covered with blankets. So, I shook him again.

"Get up, please! I have to go," I begged him. He was groggy from his partying the night before.

"Go yourself!" And then he shot the F-word at me too.

I set the cup of coffee down, threw my coat around me, once more assaulted by the stabbing, gut-wrenching pain, and I walked down the stairs, slamming the door behind me. The freezing winter air smacked me in the face adding insult to injury. I didn't have a plan at all. I stood still for a second, and my tears seemed to be freezing to my eyeballs. I tried to blink them away as I pulled my coat around me a little tighter. Just then, a woman from the Bible study group (and who also had stopped attending) happened by the apartment. I flagged her down, and when she stopped her car and rolled down her window I quickly told her I had to go to the hospital.

"Get in," she said while also motioning to me to do so. God was clearly watching over me.

She dropped me off at the hospital and I found my way to the emergency room. As soon as I took care of the necessary paper work I was ushered to an operating room where I was told to strip down, get into a hospital gown and lie on a table. My blood was drawn and tested. It confirmed a miscarriage. Before long the doctor arrived and proceeded to do a D & C (dilation and curettage surgery) without giving me any anesthesia. Tears dripped down both sides of my face and hit the examination table. I could barely withstand the pain and grabbed the side of the table with my right hand and squeezed it with all my might. The nurse held my other hand while the doctor dug in deep and scraped everything out of my uterus. I couldn't speak the whole time because I was trying so hard to deal with the completely agonizing pain. After it was over I asked the nurse why I wasn't given anything for pain. I was told that there simply hadn't been enough time.

As the nurse gave me instructions for my recovery as well as various medications, I noticed that Matthew was now standing at the doorway. The hospital staff asked me if I was going home with that man and I told them that I was, without letting on about any problems. Where else could I go? He had control over me.

Back at the apartment I committed myself to bed rest. I was weak beyond anything I had ever felt before. I was crushed in spirit yet somehow determined to survive to tell the tale. I couldn't as yet fully wrap my heart around the loss of the baby. I grieved and tried to heal as best

I could. It was my second miscarriage while there at the apartment, but this one had been more intense.

Mary Showed Up

I was regaining my strength. Matthew was still busy investigating places for potential robberies to fund his drug addictions. One such place was a parish church. He wanted to steal the Oriental carpet under the altar. He continued to have drug and alcohol parties at the apartment, which made me feel sick on many levels. I was getting fed up with everything going on. I deeply yearned for spring and the hope that it could somehow bring to my heart.

One afternoon while I watched Matthew's friends deliver cases of beer to the apartment I told Matthew that I had been invited to stay overnight at a friend's house. He knew the people. I told him that I felt the cigarette smoke at the party that night would make me too sick to stay in the apartment. I must have caught him at a good time because he said it would be okay as long as I would be back in the morning.

A couple of friends who used to go to the Bible study picked me up that evening and brought me to their apartment. While there, Theo (not his real name) held up a rosary, and I stared at it, mesmerized. The rosary swung gently from his hand, glistening with the light that filtered through the kitchen window. Theo had found it earlier that day and said that for some reason he thought he should show it to me. He wasn't Catholic, and the rosary didn't mean much to him. Still he seemed to be fascinated with it. I asked him if I could hold it, and he told me to take it for the night. I was thankful that Theo had cooperated with an inspiration to show it to me.

Years later I would be visiting Theo behind bars. He had been arrested for possession of drugs with intent to sell and sentenced to a few years in a high-security prison.

Yet it was through Theo that Mother Mary showed up totally unexpectedly in my life. As I lay in bed that night, I squeezed the rosary beads passionately, as if by clutching them tightly enough Mary would suddenly pop into the room to save me. Memories of my mother drawing her eight kids together to pray the Rosary in front of a statue of the Blessed Virgin came to mind. With the beads close to my heart, I prayed that I could get to sleep. Though I knew I was safe there, it took quite a while to relax. Other than my night in Texas, this was the only other time I had been away from the apartment at night. I was riddled with guilt for not being at the apartment with Matthew. At the same time, I was filled with a kind of rage about what was going on over there and also struggling with intense fear about my entire situation. I finally drifted off.

I awoke startled, wondering where I was and then instantly remembering that I had to go back to Matthew. I pulled the rosary to my heart again and whispered a prayer. I had a quick breakfast and gave the beads back to Theo before returning to my imprisonment.

Snap

The presence of Mother Mary in my life again was a welcome and heartening companionship indeed. I no longer had possession of the rosary but I clung to the memory of holding it that night. Even so, my mind was cluttered with all that went on at the apartment—I was constantly distracted. Fear had me bound tightly in chains. In the deepest recesses of my heart lay the ever-present worry that if I slipped up Matthew would kill my family as he had threatened.

One day when I was sitting near the bay window in the living room, Matthew came rushing in from the kitchen. With a crazed look spread across his face, he ran over to me, shoved a pistol into my hands, and thrust his head onto my lap. He squeezed my hands around the gun and forced my finger into the opening for the trigger.

"Shoot me, Donna! You're killing me! Just do it—get it over with! Kill me!"

I struggled with all my might to resist him as he pushed my finger toward the trigger.

"Jesus, Jesus, Jesus, help me please, Jesus!" I cried. Actually, I felt like I was screaming but the words came out quietly as tears poured down my face. In all my life, I had never experienced such terror. Nor had I ever called out to Jesus as desperately. Death was there, right in my lap, and yet it never entered my mind that if Matthew were dead, if I were forced to kill him, my present troubles would be over. I would be free of him.

But, I couldn't kill anyone—I wouldn't.

Jesus did help me. He immediately came to my rescue, answering the frantic desperate prayer I cried out to Him. Matthew suddenly got off my lap and hurled the gun to where it hit the wall and fell to the floor. He screamed some obscenities as he rushed out of the room like a maniac. I remained seated in the chair, paralyzed. I don't know how long I sat there, scared out of my mind. I was praying, trembling, and crying silently. I knew I had to be very careful of my every move, sound, and even breath so as not to agitate Matthew in any way.

As much as I wanted to run like mad out of there, I knew that fleeing then was not an option. He would overtake me in no time. Matthew had expressed something he had never said to me before: I was "killing" him. I couldn't possibly guess what he meant by that or what was going on inside of him. I thought he might have realized that I did not want to be with him.

Matthew came back to the room, picked up the gun, and stuck it in his pocket. Even though his behavior had been traumatic for me, I knew I had to act as if I cared about Matthew so that I could regain his trust and eventually plan my escape. It would have been very easy for me to give in to fear and give up on hope, but I had to hope that one day I would get out of there safely and that my family would remain safe too.

Finally Spring Arrived

When spring arrived, Matthew said he was going away for a couple of days to buy some cream-of-the-crop drugs. It would be the first time he left me alone for that long. He assured me that his friends would be keeping an eye on the apartment and would be reporting to him. In other words, I was going to be watched.

God gave me the strength and courage to start planning my escape. I didn't know exactly when Matthew would leave. It depended upon his mood and when the drugs were ready, among other things. I couldn't ask him about it because I didn't want him to suspect anything.

Matthew said good-bye to me early one morning just before he left on his trip. He would be taking the old car and leaving me without transportation. His rifles and machine gun were in his arms covered with a blanket. His handgun was in the small camouflage canvas bag that hung from his shoulder. Apparently he was leaving me without weapons too.

I got out of bed quickly and dressed. I gathered some of my things and put them into a plastic garbage bag. I grabbed a few items of clothing from the closet and threw them in the bag too. Then I tossed the bag under the bed just until I could be sure that Matthew was really gone. The last thing I wanted was for him to come back into the apartment and catch me packing. God only knows what would have happened then.

I ate breakfast and waited. I couldn't leave yet because he might have driven around the block, testing to see what I would do.

I contacted a few friends who were willing to help me. My plan was to stay at various places, constantly moving about for a while like a gypsy. I didn't say anything to my family as yet because I wasn't sure my plan would work and wanted to keep them safe.

At last I figured I had waited long enough. The morning was a good time to leave, I thought, since Matthew's friends would most likely not be in the area until later that evening. The plastic bag containing my belongings was small enough. If I were caught or seen I would say I was bringing the trash outside.

I took a quick look around the apartment, walking from room to room. I glanced at the chair I sat in when Matthew tried to get me to blast his brains out on my lap. I peered in the bedroom where I suffered the terrible miscarriage.

I was ready. I turned the lock from the inside and closed the door behind me. I hurried down the back stairs and stood before the back door for a minute, catching my breath. I felt strange leaving the apartment on my own. Even more, I felt afraid. But I was going to open the door to my freedom no matter what. I was going to get out of there.

I opened the back door slightly and looked all around. Nothing unusual appeared to be happening so I stepped out, closed the door behind me, and quickly walked through the alley and up the street where I would meet my ride. I never looked back. I walked as quickly as I could, looking down at my feet, hoping no one would notice me.

My friends waiting at the top of the hill picked me up and drove me to my first hideout, which was only a few miles from the apartment. There I saw the familiar faces I knew from the Bible study meetings I had attended.

That first night sleeping at a friend's house was a bit strange for me, but I felt mostly safe. I was thinking that Matthew would still be driving to his out-of-state destination and would most likely not have a reason to call the apartment. Those were the days of pay phones and not cell phones. The following day I grew more anxious and concerned that I would be found out by him or his friends. I tried to keep a very low profile and stayed in the house.

I was moved to another location a couple of weeks later. It was a house owned by the community that ran the Bible study. Again, I saw familiar people at this house and felt basically safe there.

One night in my room I was awakened from a sound sleep when someone climbed on top of me. Was it a nightmare about Matthew? No, it was a man at the Christian house who was raping me. I tried to push him off me, but to no avail. After he finished his transgression, he started to cry. He collapsed into a heap on the floor beside my bed and sobbed like a baby. "I'm sorry!" he blurted out.

I was so shocked I was speechless. I was furious that this could happen to me in a Christian house, but I forgave the young man right then and there. At the same time I was ashamed of myself, even though the rape was entirely his fault. Unfortunately a lot of rape victims feel this way. We ended up agreeing that we would both pray I wouldn't become pregnant. I didn't tell anyone at the house what had happened, but I asked to be transferred to another location.

Moving On

I moved from place to place like a nomad for several months. I went to the Bible study once in a while, and I also went to confession and Mass. I did not hear from Matthew, and I believed that God was protecting me and my family.

I had been in touch with my parents to assure them that I was okay, but I had not yet told them the whole story. I moved into another apartment, got a job, and got together with friends in my spare time. Bit by bit I was reclaiming my life. I didn't expect to get back the belongings I had left in the apartment, but I didn't care the least bit about that. I just wanted to be me again.

One day, as I was getting ready to leave my apartment building, a delivery man came to the door holding a large white box addressed to me. I opened the box hurriedly to find a dozen bright red roses. My heart jumped. I opened the card. It was signed by Matthew! I froze for a moment.

How did he find me? I wondered.

I thought about calling the police, but feared I would get into trouble for Matthew's crimes. I also feared Matthew; he still had a hold on my mind.

His note said that he loved me and that he wanted to take me to dinner and to the ocean. He knew I was fond of the ocean because we had gone there together when we had first started to date. I was almost tempted to say yes because I feared I might have to continue some kind of charade for my safety or my family's.

His note asked me to call him, but I forced myself not to. When I didn't hear anything more from Matthew, I figured he had given up on me and tried to put him out of my mind.

Then, months later, Matthew suddenly showed up. I was standing outside my apartment chatting with a friend, when I recognized the all-too-familiar figure sauntering up the sidewalk with his handgun pouch on his shoulder.

As Matthew walked determinedly toward me, I tried not to panic and stood completely motionless. Sensing trouble, my friend slowly walked a couple of steps to the right.

When he was only about an arm's length from me, Matthew stopped, planted his feet, and looked right into my eyes.

"Do you love me?" he asked. "Are you coming back to me?"

Oh my God! Please help me. Please! I prayed under my breath.

There was no escaping his penetrating stare or the fact that his hand rested on the bag over his shoulder. It took every bit of strength I could muster and then some to answer, "No."

"No," I repeated, in case my first answer was inaudible and also because I needed to say it again.

Miraculously, without a word, Matthew slowly turned around and walked away. Thank God he didn't react violently. I was astonished that he didn't.

Once I recovered from the shock of seeing Matthew again, I took a deep breath and exhaled slowly. Finally the chains that had bound me to him were broken. The freedom to move forward was both comforting and scary.

After that fateful day, I didn't talk about the time I had spent in that apartment—to anyone. Eventually, years later, I told a few people. The exact amount of time I was there is unknown to me, even to this day. Time is a hard thing to judge when one is in that sort of intense survival mode. But spring had arrived, and the hope of new life was ushering me forth.

5

My Vocation: Joy amid Misery

The brightest ornaments in the crown of the blessed in heaven are the sufferings which they have borne patiently on earth.

— Saint Alphonsus Maria de Liguori

I tried to forget the horrid past and to move forward. But what was forward? Where should I head? What would I do? I inched along.

"You'd better put your shoes on or else you might cut your feet on broken glass," the bartender warned me. I was barefoot in a biker's bar. Would my father's instructions about wearing shoes ever sink in? How I started going to that place, I really can't remember. But it became a regular hangout. I usually went there with a friend, sometimes by myself. I managed to get a ride there and back because I didn't have a car.

Soon after arriving, a glass of wine or a double shot of gold tequila would be at my place at the bar. The bartender had taken a liking to me, and I never had to pay for drinks. I would down two or three double shots of tequila without a problem. If I had any more than that, I would be in the ladies' room puking my guts out while the walls spun around. Unfortunately, I had learned that lesson the hard way. One experience like that was enough for me!

One night the bartender and his friend took me to their place for the night. I didn't have a ride home and agreed that I would stay the night there and go back to my apartment the following day.

"You know, Donna, we could just take you into the woods and rape you and then kill you," the bartender's friend said with a sappy smile. Since I knew he was joking, I did not realize until much later how vulnerable I was then. I was unaware of the risks I was taking in the company I was keeping.

I was trying to figure out who I was and what to do with my new-found freedom. Not having exercised any control over my situation for so long, having lived only to please or appease others, I went a little far in the other direction. I'm glad to say, though, that my bar-hopping phase ended quickly, but not before I worked as a bartender at a very popular disco. It was a trendy spot, where I learned to make most mixed drinks in a very short amount of time. The manager who hired me gave me a few hours of training and then left me to fend for myself on a busy Friday night. He went out to do his own partying and came back a few hours later. The whole time I was filling nonstop orders from people lined up all around the rectangular bar, clamoring for drinks. Talk about being thrown into the fire!

The Page Turns

After the disco, I got a job at a sandwich shop and began to settle down a bit. I was in regular touch with my family, and occasionally I went to Bible study, although after some weird things happened in that crowd I stopped going. When not working I spent time with my friends including my new boyfriend, Chris (not his real name), whom I had met at a Christian coffee house. Chris and I started to see a lot of each other and eventually dated.

One day, Chris popped the question.

"Will you marry me?"

He didn't have a ring, and for a minute I wasn't exactly sure if he was serious. When I realized he was in earnest, I accepted his proposal. At nineteen going on twenty I felt more like thirty. I felt as though I had spent ten years with Matthew, and seemed older than I was. Marrying Chris seemed like the right thing for me, and my parents approved.

Chris and I bought fifteen-dollar wedding rings at a hippie jewelry shop and made plans to be married in about a year. That time frame soon seemed too long, and we decided on an earlier date. Chris wanted to tie the knot even sooner, but I told him I needed time to plan the wedding. I made my vintage-style wedding dress, which had lots of old-fashioned lace. I even made Chris' suit, which was white as he requested.

We got married during a blizzard. It was such intense weather that I don't even know how we got to the church safely, and for that matter, how anyone else did. We were young and foolish, and oblivious to the storm. So were our guests, apparently, because everyone who was invited showed up.

We managed to secure a small loan from a relative to take a honeymoon in Europe, where we stayed for a month, traveling from country to country on trains. We lived very cheaply, having purchased in advance inexpensive train passes that allowed us to jump on any Western European train at any time. We stayed in modest pensions, so that we could enjoy the rich cultures and breathtaking sights. We toured several countries, including Belgium, Switzerland, France, Germany, and the Netherlands.

The blissful European adventure came to an end, and we were back in the United States searching for employment. We no longer had a vehicle because the friend who used our car while we were in Europe abandoned it on the White Stone Bridge when it broke down there. Before we got married Chris had worked in a little French bistro, so after our honeymoon he went back there. I got a job there as well. It was enjoyable work, and we became friendly with the owners and the familiar patrons. But we were struggling quite a bit financially. One day I opened the refrigerator and the pantry and could find only two carrots, an onion, and a potato. That was it. I steamed them and we ate them for dinner that night.

After a while we decided we should try to earn a better income, so we registered with a New York City agency to secure a live-in position with an affluent family. We were twenty and twenty-three years old— unheard-of ages for a housekeeper and a chef—but we managed to snag a job and in no time were living and working in a mansion in Greenwich, Connecticut, earning more money than ever before.

The couple we worked for told us repeatedly that they appreciated our meals and housekeeping. Each day we cleaned every bathroom, dusted and vacuumed every room, fluffed every pillow, and scrubbed the kitchen to perfection. We ordered everything that was needed for the household and did the grocery shopping as well. Each day we put out a feast for their dinner. We also learned the art of keeping a steak medium rare while we waited for the master of the house to arrive home on his private jet.

Not too long after beginning our job in Greenwich, I found out I was expecting a baby. I was very excited about the discovery, but I didn't feel well physically. I went about my duties as if I were fine, hiding my morning sickness and fatigue, because I didn't want to tell our employers about the pregnancy. I feared they would be upset since they had recently hired us. It was tough when the lady of the house curtly complained about a wrinkle on her husband's collar and said I needed to be more diligent with my ironing in the future. With pregnancy hormones raging, I had half a mind to say something, but I bit my tongue instead.

"Yes, ma'am."

One time though, I almost lost my temper with her. She complained about the laundry, and as soon as she was finished I gently but firmly explained that the washer and dryer were not working properly. She was amazed that I had stood up to her and immediately backed down, saying she would have the appliances fixed.

The woman rang a silver bell whenever she wanted something from me. Just when I was attempting to have my lunch or to have a short break later in the afternoon—after finishing my work, taking off my apron, and putting up my swollen feet for a bit—I would hear that horrid bell. My employer made sure she got her money's worth out of me. It turns out I would develop a love-hate relationship with bells. But, more on that later.

Thursday was our day off, and it couldn't come soon enough. We would take a taxi to the train station and head to our former town, where we stayed for the night before returning to Greenwich on Friday. It was a short respite each week, but we relished every minute we had to visit with our families.

We worked at our live-in jobs as long as we could and then gave our notice. It was becoming too much for me to keep up with the heavy housework; I needed to preserve my pregnancy and my sanity too! We left the job on good terms.

Getting Ready for Baby

We searched the ads in the newspaper for an apartment and became very weary looking for a place to call our home. One rental seemed perfect. It was a small bungalow set back from the road, and it had a nice little yard. I imagined our child playing happily there one day. But my bubble was soon burst when the owner of the house said, "No children are allowed." She had noticed my protruding abdomen. I felt violated and hurt. Why should I be treated as if I had the plague just because I was carrying a child?

Despite the setback, we finally found a nice garage apartment and moved in immediately. Chris secured a restaurant job, and I began my nesting to get ready for our baby. We picked up a secondhand crib, a little bassinette, and a dresser. I thoroughly enjoyed going to thrift shops and consignment shops (yes, I had gotten over my aversion to them) and buying itty-bitty baby clothes that I washed, folded, and put away for my little bambino. I took such delight in the miniature clothes as they floated in the breeze on the clothesline. Sometimes I opened the drawers of the little dresser and just looked at the folded clothes all ready for my baby who was growing very large inside of me. My nights were interrupted with little baby feet poking into my rib cage.

A house rental suddenly became available, and though it was challenging to move again we took the place, which was a beautiful, rustic old home in the rural area of Ridgefield where my parents lived. It was not only in the same town, but on the same road. I was so happy about that. We would have lots of privacy as it was in the woods in God's country.

Chris and I attended Lamaze childbirth classes, and I planned to have a natural delivery. I started reading up on everything about babies, their care and nurturing. After learning more about the benefits of breastfeeding and of not putting a baby on a rigid schedule, I planned to breastfeed my child on demand. About twenty and a half years old, I felt very ready to bring a little one into the world. I couldn't wait.

One afternoon my obstetrician called and instructed me to go to the hospital for a test. He told me that a certain blood level was very low (which he determined from the copious amounts of my urine that had been collected in gallon-sized containers and sent to a lab). He said the test was necessary to check the health of the baby. As we spoke I glanced out the window and observed snow coming down very hard with no sign of letting up any time soon. I questioned the need for going to the out-of-town hospital on such a snowy day. He told me it was not a choice, but a must. He added that if the tests didn't come out positively at the hospital, he would have to perform an emergency C-section.

I hung up the phone and immediately picked it up again, dialing my dear mother's number. By this point I was starting to cry. I got down on my knees by the side of my bed and prayed as I dialed. I was scared. I didn't want to undergo major surgery. I wanted a natural birth.

When my mother answered the phone, I spilled out through tears my situation and disappointment. In her steady, comforting voice she said, "Donna, you'll do anything you need to do to get that baby born safely."

I shed a few more tears and said, "No, I won't." Of course, I would follow my doctor's instructions; I only said that because I was frightened and knew I could be completely honest with my mother. After she promised her prayers, I thanked her and hung up the phone. I remained kneeling beside my bed for a few minutes, crying out to Jesus to help me. Then it was off to the hospital in a blizzard. This snowstorm, by the way, was so intense that it would eventually cripple the Northeast and cause even snowplows to pull off the roads. Thank God we made it to the hospital before driving became impossible.

At the hospital I was hooked up to a couple of machines to monitor my unborn baby and me. My doctor determined that my baby was in distress and needed to be delivered immediately by an emergency C-section. I was so scared of surgery and so sad that I couldn't give birth naturally, that I began to tremble.

In no time at all, I was prepped and ready for the operating room. But there was one problem. The insertion of the spinal anesthesia had failed, causing a great deal of pain. They promptly resorted to general anesthesia, which completely knocked me out. One minute I was trying to breathe under the smelly mask, and the next thing I knew I was in the recovery room and my baby had been born. After I could feel my legs and wiggle my toes, I was wheeled past the nursery on the way to my room.

The nurse stopped in front of the window and motioned to another nurse to hold up my baby. I couldn't pick up my neck, but I strained my eyes to focus. There he was, with dark hair and flailing arms, his mouth wide open, expressing his opinion about having his slumber interrupted. There was my baby. It was surreal.

When I was at last able to hold and to nurse my baby—Justin Michael would be his name—I carefully unwrapped his blanket and peered at his tiny body and spindly legs. Born ten days early at six pounds, thirteen ounces, he was nevertheless long for a newborn. I drew him up to my breast and attempted to teach him how to nurse. The drugs that had been given to me made him a bit groggy, so we needed to work at this until he caught on. And in a short while he did.

Justin was truly a miracle baby. His umbilical cord had been wrapped around his tiny neck; that's why the monitors had detected his heart slowing down. As he was born, the doctors and nurses unwrapped the cord not once, not twice, but three times to unbind him. Justin was born *just in* time (pun intended!). Thank God.

I am extremely thankful that my obstetrician (God rest his soul) was skilled and brilliant enough to insist that I go to the hospital even though a blizzard was underway. Throughout the years I have heard about many babies dying during childbirth because the cords were wrapped around their necks unbeknownst to the doctor and the mother—this is very sad indeed.

6

Motherhood Becomes Me

A living love hurts. Jesus, to prove His love for us, died on the Cross. The mother, to give to her child, has to suffer. If you really love one another properly, there must be sacrifice.

—Blessed Mother Teresa

I came home from the hospital seven days after I went in for that fateful test on that blustery January day. A long narrow path had been shoveled from the driveway to the house for our homecoming. The snow was thigh-high! Slowly I carried Justin swaddled in many blankets, and I took extra care with my footing because I didn't want to drop him!

Once inside our rental house I unwrapped little Justin, changed his diaper, then rewrapped him in a light blanket in the form of a little papoose. I asked Chris to start a fire in the fireplace. The old house was very drafty, and I wanted to be sure my little firstborn was warm enough. After the fire was underway, I sat in the rocking chair close to the fireplace and let my baby melt into my body as I kept him close to my heart. I'm sure he heard my heart beating as the chair rocked back and forth, clicking in a rhythmic motion on the bare wood. I spent endless hours holding little Justin in that rocking chair near the warm fire while classical music played quietly in the background.

When Justin stirred a bit, started to wiggle and sigh, then let out a little whimper, I brought him close to my breasts to suckle. He latched on and heartily nursed. Before long he was fast asleep again.

Now I was hungry. I gently placed Justin in the white wicker bassinette and, still hurting from the C-section, moved slowly into the chilly kitchen. On the north side of the house, the kitchen never seemed to get warm enough. In fact, we had to get a portable heater to keep it tolerable. I made myself a fried-egg sandwich, which became the main-stay of my diet because it's fairly nutritious, inexpensive, and easy to prepare, and because I had such a constant hankering for one.

I think I was born to be a mother. I thoroughly enjoyed everything about it. I was only twenty-one years old, but I felt confident in nurturing my precious baby. It was a very cold winter the year Justin was born, with lots of snow and ice. I stayed inside much of the time, unless Justin or I had a doctor's appointment, but I was content to stay in the heart of the home and care for my baby. After I healed from the surgery, I took him to Mass and on other outings.

When Justin's baptismal day arrived, he was ushered into the Church and the waters of Baptism flowed over his head. We gathered back at the house to continue our celebration.

Justin grew by leaps and bounds. He took his first steps early, at only nine months old. He was just a little tyke toddling all over our one-story wood cabin. One day when Justin was about eleven months old, I placed him on the floor after nursing him and watched him amble into the next room, where he sat down on the floor. He then stood up and headed back toward me. When he got to the doorway he slipped on the door jam and plunked down on his bottom, which was no big deal. But, what happened next was frightening.

Justin started gagging and then choking. I ran over and scooped him up, holding him sideways, gently patting his back and trying to assess the situation. He started to go limp in my arms and was turning gray-ish. I screamed for Chris to call an ambulance and immediately turned Justin upside down. For some reason, Chris chose not to call. Thank-fully, Justin vomited, and a penny came out of his mouth and onto the floor. Suddenly he regained his composure and color. I carried him over to the bed, set the penny on the nightstand, and then sat on the bed holding him, rubbing his back and trying to calm myself. I had child-proofed the house, but there must have been a stray penny on the floor that he snuck in his mouth when he was facing away from me. That single penny could have cost Justin's life! Just then Justin started to reach for the penny on the nightstand.

"Oh, no you don't!" I said. I could see that keeping my toddler safe was going to take constant vigilance!

As Justin grew and the weather got warmer, we spent a lot of time outdoors. After all, we lived in the woods of beautiful New England, rich with stunning foliage and wildlife. We took lots of walks and played in our spacious yard. One of our favorite pastimes was riding my bike down our mile-long driveway. Justin would be strapped into the kiddie seat in the back, and we would sail down the hill, watching the trees whizz by and delighting in the wind in our faces. Trudging back up that hill was another story. I would walk the bike with Justin still in his seat, kicking his feet and smiling from ear to ear.

Changing Dynamics

Chris did not adapt to family life as easily as I did. After Justin was born he grew antsy and began to withdraw from me. He stopped showing me physical affection—no hugs, no kisses, no holding hands. He told me he just couldn't. There were unexpected outbursts too. One day Chris told me that he didn't think he should have gotten married or become a father. He seemed to be very confused and a bit depressed. I thought our parish priest might be able to help him, and I asked Chris if he would speak with him. Chris reluctantly agreed, and we met with Father; but Chris was unable to speak freely about what was troubling him. Father advised us as best he could, but the meeting did not accomplish much.

The more Chris talked about not wanting to be married, the more I reminded him that we had brought a child into the world and that he deserved a mother and a father. One day I took out our wedding photos and placed them all around the house. You couldn't miss them. I wanted to snap Chris out of the mysterious mental state that was drowning him. I didn't know if the photos could do any good, but I felt I had to try something. I also prayed for help.

I could no longer count on Chris on many fronts. He was constantly quitting or getting fired from his jobs. There was never enough money to pay the bills, to pay the rent, to buy food. Fortunately I was nursing Justin, and so at least he was well fed. I was another story. I needed to eat well so that I could provide nourishment for my baby.

I started working part-time in the evenings at a local restaurant to try to supplement our income. It wasn't a lot but it helped to buy groceries. When I worked the lunch shift occasionally, my parents—who were getting on in age—were able to watch Justin for short periods of time.

There were nights when Chris would come home very late. An hour or two would pass after he should have been home, and I would have no way to get in touch with him to know if he was okay. This was before cell phones were invented. To make matters worse, he had taken a job with a private painting contractor who rarely paid him on time. His pay was never consistent. His work hours weren't either.

One night as it was getting very late, I became frantic because Chris hadn't come home. I called his boss' number and there was no answer. I took care of little Justin—got him bathed and fed and into bed—and then I just sat, prayed, and waited. Hours passed. Finally, the front windows lit up from headlights coming into the driveway, and I rushed out the door to greet Chris. He got out of the old borrowed truck that we used as our vehicle and shuffled a couple of steps toward the house. He was as drunk as could be. It was a miracle that he had made it home in one piece.

I was extremely upset to see him in this state and was fearful too as a sad reality settled into my brain. I was married to a man with a serious drinking problem. He did not have this problem when we were dating and first married. Perhaps the weight of responsibilities on his shoulders was too much for him. I don't know. I certainly did not understand alcoholism at that time, and I stood there paralyzed for a moment, feeling really scared in the depths of my being. I told Chris that I was very upset because I hadn't been able to reach him by phone and that when he didn't come home I was very worried about him, pointing out the fact that we had a little baby for whose sake he needed to stop drinking to excess. Though I was upset, I hugged him. He said he didn't think I would want a hug from him. Perhaps my hug was an attempt to hold onto our marriage for I felt it was falling apart.

We went inside, and I quickly ushered him to the bathroom because he said he had to vomit. Then I stayed with him, holding his head up over the toilet bowl until he was finished puking. I helped him get to bed and then stayed awake most of that night. I was frightened and not sure how to cope with this serious problem.

Being continually late with our rent did not sit well with our landlords, who were getting fed up with us. Each payday Chris came home carrying a six-pack of beer and popping one open as soon as he got into the house. I later learned that he bought two extra bottles of beer in addition to the six-pack, which he would drink while driving home. So, he was pretty well primed by the time he walked through the door. Then being in an irritable mood, he would start picking on me. Reasonable conversations about the bills, or anything else for that matter, are not possible with someone who is drunk, so it became harder and harder for us to communicate.

Chris lost another job and sunk into another depression. The landlords were not happy about my husband's lack of employment and didn't mince words when approaching us about it. Since they lived on the same piece of property, we had to see them constantly. Mainly I was the one who dealt with their complaints. Chris was usually watching television or napping.

Somehow we survived. During one particularly trying time our parish priest sent over a couple of bags of canned goods because he thought we might need some help.

Justin had gotten a great start at our house in the country, but eventually we were forced to move out when the rent was raised and we could no longer afford it. We found an affordable apartment in a neighboring city, and we moved in by making several trips in the old pickup truck loaded with boxes of our belongings. We settled into our apartment on the second floor of a two-family home, complete with lots of ugly cheap paneling throughout. I decorated it and made it our own as much as possible, and Justin and I enjoyed swinging on a swing set at the local park whenever we could.

Chris secured another restaurant job, and I worked part-time at a restaurant in the evenings and on the weekends whenever Chris or my parents could take care of our son. It was a juggling act trying to help with the finances and to raise Justin properly.

Losing My Father

Although my father was only in his sixties, his health had been deteriorating. He suffered from a heart attack and then a stroke that left him paralyzed on one side of his body. Seeing him struggle to get his words out was very sad. In addition to cardiovascular disease, he had diabetes and eventually needed to have one of his toes and part of his foot amputated because of gangrene. In time my dad recovered his speech and nearly the full use of the side of his body affected by the stroke. The doctors were surprised by his improvement. I felt that God had given my father another year of life with my mother—a year for forgiveness and tenderness perhaps. My mother took very good care of her husband throughout his illnesses. Dad seemed very happy and took each day as it came. I was ecstatically happy that he had returned to the sacraments and was back in the graces of the Church.

Then one day he suffered another heart attack and was rushed to the hospital. It didn't look promising. I felt I should prepare my son for my father's possible death because it seemed imminent. I took a walk with Justin and told him that Grandpa was very sick and that he was probably going to die soon.

Soon after, I received a phone call informing me that my father had died. I wished I could have been there with him before he closed his eyes on this world, but I knew he was in God's hands. Chris, who hadn't shown me any affection for some two years, surprisingly gave me a hug of sympathy.

The night of my father's death I woke up to a strange sight: standing before me at the foot of my bed was my father, white and all aglow. I had no doubt that it was he. *Is it a dream? Is God showing me that my father is safe with Him?*

Months later, one evening after we had eaten a spaghetti dinner, Chris started to choke. He had finished eating his last bite and immediately lit up a cigarette. I don't think he had fully swallowed his food when he inhaled a puff of the cigarette, which caused the food to lodge in his windpipe. He couldn't breathe. I felt petrified. I had never done the Heimlich maneuver, nor was I ever taught how to do it, but I had seen it pictured on a poster in the kitchen of one of the restaurants where I had worked.

I got behind Chris, wrapped my arms around him and gave a good thrust under his diaphragm below his rib cage. It didn't work. He still couldn't breathe! Soon he crumpled and fell to the floor. He was beginning to pass out. I screamed out the window for my downstairs neighbors to come and help me. The screaming was useless; they weren't home. I was terrified. I got down on the floor and tried to get behind Chris to do the maneuver again. *Please, Jesus, help me!* Finally, Chris vomited and the windpipe cleared. Thank God the maneuver worked!

At some point we moved again, to another apartment in the same town. I dreaded packing everything all over again and having to settle once more in a new area. But such was life for us. Justin started in a community preschool and thoroughly enjoyed mingling with the children and learning. I took a job as a security guard at a large corporation while Justin was at school.

Along Came Baby Number Two

"We knew she'd do this!"

So said some of Chris' relatives, along with other hurtful comments, when we broke the news that I was expecting another baby. As if it takes only one person to make a baby! Besides, Justin was already more than four years old. They just didn't understand my openness to life. I would try not to let their remarks bother me.

Despite the negativity from some people, I was extremely happy to be expecting again. I was also happy about another big step for our family, something we had been pondering awhile: moving to Texas. Relatives had been suggesting that we move there to be closer to them, and we decided the time was right.

My family in Connecticut was very sad to see us leave, but Chris and I thought it would be good for us to get a new start in a brand new place. We would get out of the city and enjoy life on a farm. What could be better? We rented a huge truck, said our tearful good-byes, and took off for Texas. In addition to all of our belongings, we took our cat, dog, and rabbit.

For the first two months we lived with relatives. The two families lived on small farms in rural Texas where the sky was wide and the snakes were big! I had never seen flying roaches until we moved to Texas, nor had I ever seen real scorpions before.

Unfortunately, the scorpions we saw were inside the house. We always had to be mindful of what might be inside our shoes before we put them on, as well as where we stepped, whether inside the house or out. A couple of times I was attacked by fire ants, which quietly crawl up one's feet and legs and then, once in a comfy spot, sting all at once. The attack feels like being burned—hence the name.

Time to Pray

Life on the farm provided me with hours and hours of time to pray in silence as my unborn baby stirred within me and Justin played nearby. I often sat outside on an old folding lawn chair. When the sun became too hot, I moved my chair into the shade of a nearby tree and read and prayed some more. I was also given time to read about the lives of many of the saints. God was working on my heart, and I felt that I was growing closer to Him.

We found a rental house a few towns away from our relatives and along the route to the hospital where I would be delivering our baby in about six months. We moved our boxes and furniture in. Each day Chris went off to his job at the tire shop, which was about an hour away, while I stayed home unpacking. Justin enjoyed playing outside in our little yard, although every day I had to pull a dozen or so ticks off him.

The house was a mess of boxes and household items, but I was determined to make it a home for us. We had permission to fix up the place; so after putting away most of the necessary things, I decided to tackle the living room wallpaper, which was tattered and peeling off the walls. I grabbed an end of the brittle yellowed paper and gave it a good yank. The flimsy paper tore away from the wall in pieces, and I was instantly horrified by what I found. Not only were there gaping holes in the wood rotting inside the walls, there were nests of roaches—massive nests! Disturbed by my intrusion, the roaches came pouring out. There were hundreds and hundreds of them! I grabbed some nearby window cleaner and started spraying them as quickly as I could.

If that wasn't enough to make me squeamish, I soon came upon another little surprise. When I opened up the boxes of kitchenware we had stowed at a storage unit the past two months, armies of ants came marching out, running over my hands and my new kitchen too. I grabbed the pots and pans and threw them into the sink, where I doused them with hot water and washed the dead ants down the drain. I stamped all over the ants scurrying across the floor and into any opening or crevice they could find. Though the darting ants were repulsive, I'm smiling now, glad that no one caught sight of me doing this dance!

To make matters worse, the refrigerator (or, rather our food inside) wasn't safe from roaches determined to get inside. They managed to squeeze past the old rubber gaskets around the doors. It was disgusting. We couldn't afford to buy our own refrigerator, so we had to put up with the one that was provided.

The days and nights were very hot and humid in our area of Texas. Being pregnant and overheated, I was sweating from places on my body I didn't know could sweat. We didn't have air conditioning, or even a simple fan, until one day we splurged and purchased a little oscillating fan, which we carried with us from room to room. I vividly remember standing in front of the little fan one evening so that it would blow on my face while the nearby thermometer registered 100 degrees Fahrenheit. That was a drop from the 115 degrees it had reached earlier in the day. Still, 100 degrees inside the house was too hot for me.

Texas was just not my cup of tea. The people were wonderful, but the climate didn't agree with me. Before long, Chris and I began trying to figure out an exit plan. We had no savings, but we were desperate to return to Connecticut. A generous aunt aware of our predicament sent us some emergency money so that we could rent a truck and go back home. We were ecstatic!

Six months after we made the long journey to Texas with a little boy, an unborn baby, a cat, a dog, and a rabbit, we bid Texas goodbye and were on our way back home to Connecticut with all of the above except for the dog that, to our sorrow, had been killed when she was hit by a car. It was a very long way back home and it took us several days, but we grew more and more excited with each passing mile.

I wanted to surprise my mother, so I hadn't told her we were coming back. Once we arrived in Connecticut, her house was the very first place we stopped. She was overjoyed when she saw me at her front door. We ended up staying with her for a few weeks while we looked for a place to live. All the siblings and relatives were happy to have us back. How good it was to breathe in the Connecticut air and to see familiar places again!

We registered at my mother's parish and began attending Mass there. We soon found an apartment in a two-family house in a fairly quiet neighborhood, where I began feathering a new nest. I unpacked our boxes of belongings, arranged and rearranged our furniture (with help), washed all of the baby clothes Justin had worn, and set up an area for the new baby near our bed. I also shopped at thrift and consignment stores. It was such an exciting time. I was counting my blessings, happy that we didn't have to deal with any bugs in the apartment. We had left them behind in Texas where they belonged.

As the baby's due date drew near, I begged my doctor to let me deliver naturally. Considering me an educated patient, he said I could try for a natural birth unless he thought the baby was too big for that. The concern was that the bigger the baby, the greater the risk that the birth process would tear open the scar from the previous incision, which would cause serious complications. (I suspect the concern has a lot more to do with lawsuits than anything else, to tell you the truth.)

I didn't eat ice cream cones every day as my mother had when pregnant with me. Nevertheless, the doctor estimated that my baby would be about seven pounds at birth, so I would need to deliver by C-section after all.

When Chaldea (pronounced "shall-day-a") made her grand entrance into the world, she weighed a whopping nine pounds, three and a half ounces! I hadn't needed general anesthesia for the surgery, so I was awake and aware during the delivery. Chaldea was cleaned up, swaddled in a warm blanket, and placed on my chest. Still attached to the IV and restricting medical wires, I carefully drew her up close to me and caressed her head with my fingers. The joy that exploded in my heart is difficult to put into words. I held her to my breast and she immediately nursed. My life felt so rich and blessed to have been given the gift of two living children.

Chaldea was such a light in my life. She was a happy baby, and Justin just loved her. I rocked her in the same chair in which I had rocked him, and I carried her around in a baby sack I wore. We went for many walks together out in nature. What a blessing to have a baby girl!

We didn't stay at that apartment for very long. It was too small and not in a good location. We moved to another apartment in a multi-family building in another area of town. It was much bigger and had a nice yard for the kids.

There was just one thing that made me feel uneasy about our new place—the handyman who lived in the apartment right next to us. I can't say exactly what it was about him that made me cringe inside. He seemed normal enough. He had a wife and a young child. But every time I saw him, and whenever he spoke to me, I got an apprehensive feeling in the pit of my stomach.

Many times he would show up at my door, when my husband was at work, asking if he could come in and take a look at the plumbing. I would always give some excuse why it wasn't a convenient time, because the children were napping, for instance, and would tell him that the plumbing was just fine. Even when we had some sort of problem, I never told him or let him in.

We got settled in our new home. Even though the weather was getting chilly as winter began to set in, I continued to hang my family's laundry outside on a clothesline. I didn't have a clothes dryer, and I liked natural drying anyway. To dry our clothes meant carrying a laundry basket filled with heavy wet laundry up a flight of stairs and then struggling to open an old rickety window so that I could hang the clothes on the clothesline. But that certainly beat pushing a borrowed grocery store cart for miles in earlier years when I brought my clothes to the Laundromat. Shortly after we moved in, our upstairs neighbor referred to me as a "country bumpkin" behind my back because I hung our laundry outside.

My Mother's Illness

When Chaldea was a little more than a year old, my mother went to her doctor for a routine physical and found out that she had a spot in her throat that the doctor wanted to check further. After a few tests she was told that she had lung cancer. She had never smoked. My father had died about two and a half years before, and my mother had sold the house and moved to another town closer to family. I think Mom had been lonely ever since Dad's death. They had been married forty-two years. They were tough years raising eight kids through thick and thin—mostly thin—but their last year together was filled with love and forgiveness.

Chemotherapy was started for my mother immediately. Soon after, she was admitted to the hospital for various infections and setbacks. Her health was deteriorating. No more red lipstick to brighten her looks and no more outings, not even to church. She was too tired and too sick. She would be in and out of the hospital several times during the next six months. She wasn't getting better. Her cancer was insidious and merciless.

Once when I was visiting my mother at the hospital and holding eighteen-month-old Chaldea in my arms, I lifted my baby over my mother's bed rail so that she could kiss her granddaughter before we left for the night. I gave Mother a kiss too, and she teared up.

"I won't be alive to see her growing up," she cried.

Then we both cried, though I tried not to. My mother believed and hoped that in the next life she would be aware of Chaldea's growing up, but she was speaking from the here and now. She knew in her heart that she would be leaving us behind soon, and she was finally expressing it.

Another bout of pneumonia came to bully her. She fought hard against the intruder, but the chemotherapy had weakened her immune system.

Earlier my mother had declared that when she got home from the hospital she was going to take out her good china from the cabinet and use it. We shouldn't wait for special occasions, she had said, we needed to enjoy it now. But Mother wasn't able to use her good china ever again. She never came home from the hospital.

I was at home when I received the phone call informing me that my mother had died. I knew it would happen someday, but still I could not fathom the reality of it as I got in my car and hurried over to the hospital. I arrived to see my grandmother, my mother's sister Aunt Bertha, and a few others gathered in my mother's room. As I started to pass through the doorway, I froze—I could not take another step. My body would not budge. A nurse came to my side and encouraged me to approach Mom's bed.

"She's still warm," she said.

She didn't understand my hesitation. I wasn't afraid that my mother wouldn't still be warm. That's not why I stopped in the doorway. My mother had died! I had not yet come to terms with that fact. The nurse put her arm around my waist and ushered me forward. I made it to my mother's side and kissed her. Then I cried.

My mother's funeral was sad indeed, but God's grace got me through it. Many times, for months afterward, I would start to pick up the phone to call her and then sadly remember that she wouldn't be there to answer it.

An Unspeakable Gut Feeling

One day I heard the screech of a car's tires right outside our apartment. I looked out the window to see that a car had hit our little dog. With Chaldea safely strapped in her high chair, I ran out to the road and scooped up our dog from the middle of the road. He was bleeding profusely with a huge gaping wound in his side. I ran inside the apartment and grabbed a blanket to wrap around him. The handyman, Donald, (not his real name) came to the door. He had seen what had happened and offered to give me a ride in his truck to get our dog to the veterinarian's office. There was no time to feel apprehensive; I had to get our poor dog to the vet immediately. Donald helped to put Chaldea's car seat in his truck. I put Chaldea in her seat and climbed in next to her, holding our dog tightly and attempting to comfort him. The dog did not make it.

Despite his act of kindness, my uneasiness around Donald persisted. Through the walls of our apartment, I would often hear his little two-year-old boy crying. I would see Donald and his wife get in their car and drive away while leaving their son in the apartment. They said they were going to play bingo. At first I thought there might be a babysitter with the boy, but then I began to observe carefully, intending to alert the authorities if indeed the boy was left alone. I finally called to report that a two-year-old child was being left alone for long periods of time, and I was told by state authorities that they would not investigate unless I could actually see abuse happening. I told them that I could hear the boy crying and that I could see his parents leaving the building. But no, they wouldn't help.

Some months later, a detective showed up at my front door and asked if he could talk to me about Donald. He also talked to one of our neighbors. I was more than happy to help because I had always suspected that something was not right with the man, and I was very concerned for their child. This detective made several visits to our home and wanted to know if we had access to the locked garage on the property. There were certain tools he was looking for—all linked somehow to Donald. After those mysterious visits I was even more careful not to get stuck alone with Donald. I avoided him like the plague.

A few years later, I read in the local newspaper that Donald had been arrested and was serving time in prison for committing a horrendous crime. I shuddered as I read the gory details. While working in our apartment building, Donald also had been employed as a handyman at an apartment building in a neighboring town. His fingerprints on a coffee cup and other pieces of incriminating evidence helped to prove that Donald had brutally raped and killed a woman in her apartment. God rest her soul.

The news report made me appreciate that peculiar gut feeling I had experienced all along about that odd man who constantly tried to gain entrance to my apartment. To this day I am very thankful that I never let Donald into my home.

Moving Again

The time came for us to move yet again, this time to another apartment in the same town. By now I was pretty much an expert in packing and moving, though I dreaded every minute of it. It wasn't easy on any of us to move around so much. We managed by God's grace and a good dose of determination.

This new home was the lower floor of a two-family home. The landlords lived upstairs. We had a backyard for the kids—and for a dog in case we decided to get another one. There was another small house in the back. We found out later that a drug dealer lived there, which explained why lots of cars came and went at all hours.

In the spring I planted a little vegetable garden that wrapped around the house. Justin and Chaldea liked to help me in the garden. Chaldea was fascinated by the earthworms and would pick them up and investigate them. Sometimes we picked pea pods (with clean hands!) and popped the delicious peas into our mouths—right there in the garden.

We had some trouble with our landlady. There was a leak in our ceiling and water was pouring into our living room; the ceiling was breaking apart and falling down in places. When I phoned the landlady about it, the woman came flying downstairs to my apartment and started yelling, telling me she wasn't going to be responsible for our carpet or television set that were under the leak. She yanked at the carpet and pulled the television in another direction.

The landlady eventually sold the house, which spared us from further harassment from her. New tenants moved in upstairs.

Seeking Holiness

Whenever I could arrange it, I went to my parish church and kept company with Jesus in the Blessed Sacrament for as long as I could. *Here I am Lord.* I prayed much while there and came to know our Lord even more personally. We had many heart-to-heart conversations. I looked forward to any time I could have alone in prayer so long as the children were accounted for. I often took them to daily Mass. Even though they were fidgety and inattentive at times, I knew in my heart that God was granting them graces at holy Mass.

Around this time I became involved in the pro-life movement with a few fellow parishioners and friends. I often peacefully picketed at a nearby abortion facility, praying the Rosary and offering assistance and alternatives to the women going in for abortions. I usually went once a week and brought the children with me. One time a young man there was so irritated that he threatened to kill me and used many choice words to express it. Another time, a young couple allowed me to speak to them through their open car window. I crouched down to see them and eventually knelt on the pavement to be at their eye level. By the end of the conversation, they had changed their minds. The fear that had plagued them had lifted. They said they would work it out—they would have their baby! They heartily thanked me and drove away.

Once when I was at the abortion facility with my children, a car sped over part of the sidewalk and came very close to hitting us. My spiritual director Father Bill said it was too dangerous to bring my children to the abortion clinic and told me to pray at home instead. After many years of sidewalk counseling, I followed his wise advice and stopped going, but I missed praying there with my friends.

When I could devote some time to pro-life efforts, I wrote letters to the editor of the local newspaper to raise awareness about the dignity and the sanctity of human life. Sometimes I was able to get together with like-minded people at conferences. I met some Catholics who were part of the Third Order of Saint Dominic. After some time, another Catholic friend and I decided to take lessons to become members of the Third Order and to get permission to open up a branch at our parish. Before long there were many others interested in joining the group. We were blessed to have someone I considered a very wise spiritual director to guide us—Father Bill. I served as a mistress of novices and another time as the prioress. One of the apostolates of the group was to help with pro-life issues and situations.

Around that same time I heard that there was a young single mother who had no place to live. Her mother had abandoned her several years earlier. No one seemed to want her. As my friend told me about the girl, I was pondering what I could possibly do to help. Could I offer her a home? My friend encouraged me to become a licensed foster care mother so that I could take her in. I prayed about it, talked to Chris, and consulted with my spiritual director. In a short while I was an official foster mother and welcomed sixteen-year-old Bianca (not her real name) to our home.

Three-year-old Chaldea graciously and unselfishly gave up her bedroom to make room for Bianca and her baby, Sarah. It would be so special to help this young woman to get on her feet. It would be exciting to have a baby in the house too!

Speaking of babies, I found out I was expecting our third! I was a few weeks along when Bianca moved into Chaldea's bedroom. We set up a crib for baby Sarah and tried to make them both feel comfortable. My job was to teach Bianca mothering and housekeeping skills. She began to confide in me and to feel very comfortable with us.

Bianca decided to have Sarah baptized. I was to be her godmother and a friend of ours the godfather. What a glorious day it was to initiate little Sarah into the Church.

One day as we went into the parish church for Sunday Mass, Bianca told me that she was feeling very sick and thought she had the flu. We got through Mass and drove home. I checked Bianca for a fever but she didn't have one. I made her a cup of chamomile tea and encouraged her to rest. We would keep an eye on her and if need be, take her to the doctor the following day.

Later on that afternoon, Bianca confessed that she was pretty sure she was pregnant again. She was right. After a doctor's appointment a couple of days later it was confirmed that she had come to us with not just one baby, but also another on the way!

Life Is Precious

Life was busy in our new home. The house was usually bustling with activity and noise too! The kids often helped Bianca by bringing her diapers, bottles, and sometimes holding baby Sarah (with assistance). Bianca was learning to cook, clean, and care for her baby.

After several months with us, it was time for Bianca and her baby to move on. The state was emancipating her so that she could have her own apartment. Though we didn't encourage her to invite her boyfriend to move in with her, I think that was her plan. Bianca thanked us for giving her a chance to get on her feet, and we said our good-byes to each other amid tears.

Shortly after that, at sixteen weeks of pregnancy, I felt sharp, agonizing pains shooting through my abdomen. I started to pass blood clots. I called my doctor and was instructed to get to the hospital right away for an ultrasound.

The technician moved the probe all over my protruding abdomen. She took her time going back and forth, pushing down harder in places, and when she had seen enough she called the doctor into the room. They both looked at the pictures and did some more scanning. After that, the doctor told me that my baby had died. He told me that my baby didn't have a heartbeat. I couldn't believe him. He had to be wrong. The ultrasound had to be wrong.

He told me that since I was so far along in the pregnancy I would need to have surgery. I would need a D & C with suction. I shuddered when he told me. If my baby were alive, that would be an abortion. How could I be sure that I should go through with that? Through tears, I asked if I could go home and think about it. I was shocked and scared. My doctor allowed me to go home with instructions to get in touch with him after I had thought about it.

All through that night I experienced excruciating pains and passed large clots of blood. I was up all night praying and trying to get through each painful contraction. The morning couldn't come fast enough. Justin went to school, and my brother's wife accompanied me to the hospital. Chaldea came along too. Sensing that something wasn't right, she cried as we passed through the hospital doors. My sister-in-law cautioned me not to pick the child up. It was tough for me, not being able to comfort my daughter, but I heeded the wise advice. I parted from the two of them to meet my doctor and to have another ultrasound. The doctor carefully studied the screen as he moved the probe over my abdomen. He paused a few times and moved the probe some more. He stopped and told me there was simply no heartbeat. My baby had died. I was incredibly saddened to hear the truth.

The doctor told me it was important to do the surgery right away, and I agreed to have the procedure immediately after the ultrasound. As I was being given general anesthesia, I was asked to count backwards.

The very next words I heard were, "Honey, you lost a lot of blood. You are going to be staying overnight." I had just opened my eyes and was in another room. I had not one, but two IV's in my arms. One was there when I went into the surgery, and the other was a new one, for a blood transfusion.

"Oh, I can't stay here. My children won't understand," I told her.

"You'll have to take that up with the doctor, Dearie."

When the doctor came to see me, I pleaded with him to let me go home. I promised that I would stay in bed and that I would get help. It was important to me to be home with the kids. I knew that Chris wouldn't be able to handle it alone. I actually feared for the children's safety.

After some more begging, the doctor chuckled and said, "Oh, all right! I'll let you go home; but be good and stay in bed, and I'll call you tomorrow."

After the transfusion was finished, I was discharged and transported home. The following day my good doctor called to check on me. I decided to ask him why every time I inhaled my chest hurt so much. That's when he told me the whole story.

"You see, Donna, as soon as you were prepped for surgery, you hemorrhaged profusely," he explained. "If that had happened in any place other than an operating room, you would not be alive today."

Then he went on to tell me what they did to save my life. The tube that was thrust down my throat to help me to breathe was the reason I felt pain with every breath now. *Wow. Life is so precious and fragile and totally not in our control!* I thought.

I kept my promise and stayed in bed for more than a week. Many friends and people I didn't know from church dropped by with casseroles and other prepared foods to help us through my convalescence. I felt very blessed to be showered with such love and care. It helped me to deal with the loss of the baby.

Later that year I learned that I was pregnant again. I had been praying for this baby. I was thrilled. My in-laws were not, however. When Chris called his mother to tell her the news, she and her live-in boyfriend suggested that I get an abortion. I was shocked and hurt, but I would be reminded of this conversation many years later.

Chris fell into another slump. He was drinking heavily and, as I found out later, taking drugs. He missed work. Communication with him was even more difficult than it had been before. Nonetheless, I got through each day the best I could, despite financial difficulties and without help from Chris. I tried to keep things light for the kids and to focus on my unborn baby.

7

Getting Behind the Wheel: Single Mom Years

Therefore I tell you, do not be anxious about your life, what you shall eat or what you shall drink, nor about your body, what you shall put on. Is not life more than food, and the body more than clothing? Look at the birds of the air: they neither sow nor reap nor gather into barns, and yet your heavenly Father feeds them. Are you not of more value than they? And which of you by being anxious can add one cubit to his span of life?

— Gospel of Matthew

One day Chris, Chaldea, and I went for a drive. Along the way, Chris seemed to become agitated. Then without warning he pulled the car over to the side of the road and simply said, "I'm leaving!" He got out of the car, stuck his thumb out to hitchhike, and got into a car that soon pulled over. Just like that! We were abandoned on the side of the road on a chilly late autumn day, when I was about a month away from giving birth to our third child.

I suspected that Chris was probably going to stay at his friend's house in New York. Prior to this, Chris and I had talked about separating temporarily. After almost ten years of marriage, and with the aid of spiritual direction, I came to believe that a separation was necessary so that Chris could get the professional help he needed to overcome his drinking problem. But I never expected that he would just abandon us suddenly on the side of the road.

Chaldea, who was buckled in the back seat, began to cry. I quickly moved to the back seat to comfort her. After a few minutes, though still in shock, I got behind the wheel, which meant moving the driver's seat back a couple of inches to make room for both me and my unborn baby. I pulled onto the road and headed straight for the welfare department.

Since my husband had just left us, there was no telling how we would support ourselves. I knew that with another C-section scheduled, I would be out of commission for some time. I was in no shape to seek employment and childcare. It just wouldn't work. I needed help—we needed help. Perhaps even more than my worries about survival at the moment, a nagging question plagued my mind: What was I going to tell Justin when he got home from school?

Asking for welfare wasn't at all easy. We had lived through tough times before; but I had never been in such a desperate situation, and I felt uncomfortable asking the government for help. I also suspected that when one is beholden to the state, one is subject to it. But I really couldn't worry about what it felt like or what it would entail. I needed help keeping a roof over our heads and food on the table

Later on I felt very awkward using food stamps to buy our family's groceries. At times, the cashier seemed to have an attitude about it. I couldn't really be sure, of course. Using the food stamps was embarrassing, and I tried to pass the stamps to the cashier quickly and discreetly.

Certainly much more difficult than applying for welfare and using its benefits, was telling Justin what had happened earlier that day. He was only nine years old. I can still remember the sorrow and confusion on his face when I told him that his dad wasn't going to be home that night and that I didn't know when he would be back. It was very difficult for us to deal with our sadness over Chris. But each morning we got out of bed and kept to our routines as best we could, and we said our prayers together.

Chris didn't visit the children for quite some time. I didn't know what I could tell them to explain why he didn't visit. I found out where Chris was staying; he was in New York with his friend as I had guessed. I called him regularly, asking him to visit the children and to provide some financial support for us. He finally came to see the children and handed me a small amount of money. He came by only a few more times. The few times that he called on the phone he was intoxicated.

One day I was beginning to feel more than my usual pregnancy fatigue, along with some dizziness. The weakness had been going on for a few days, and I figured it could be the normal tiredness a woman experiences during the last trimester. The dizziness, however, was disconcerting, so I called the doctor. After some tests, the doctor told me that I had a serious urinary tract infection and needed a double dose of strong antibiotics. He also said that I should deliver the baby about nine days earlier than my scheduled cesarean. He assured me that both the baby and I would be better off with an earlier birth. So I placed my trust in God and prayed for the best.

I felt a bit jittery as I was being prepped for my third C-section, and this one without a husband. Lying on the operating table, I wiped away a few tears as I explained my situation to the anesthesiologist. I had asked my brother's wife to be with me during the delivery, and her presence was a consolation.

Jessica Marie was born! She was beautiful and had a full head of black hair. My mother had told me that I had been born with a full head of black hair and that it was long enough for her to put a ribbon in it. Chaldea had picked out two names for her baby sister: Jessica and Rainbow Brite! Though I had pondered other names and had one ready, Chaldea's insistence on Jessica won me over. Jessica was, after all, perfect, for it means "grace from God."

I invited Chris to stay at the apartment to see the kids and to bond with Jessica. He agreed. It was a bit strange having him there, but I wanted to bring healing to our marriage and family. I had to have hope for everyone's sake. It seemed that hope was in the air with Christmas fast approaching and a beautiful new baby who was blessing our lives. As his visit was nearing an end, I asked Chris if he would stay longer. Would he consider coming back for good?

"No. I told you how long I was staying. I'm leaving as I said."

And so he left—again.

Challenges and Prayers

I shed a lot of tears when the children were asleep in bed. I didn't want them to see how upset I was. I wanted them to feel encouragement from me, so I tried to be strong. It was a very cold winter, and I was feeling particularly weak from major surgery and three kids to care for—one of them a tiny baby. I missed my mother too. I longed for spring and the warmth of sunshine on my face and the hope of better days. I had to hang on to the hope of a miracle. Some days it felt like it was all I had besides my beautiful, wonderful children.

Winter had arrived, and one evening the furnace stopped working. Even when the heat was working properly, cold air seeped through the large old window panes and the thin walls lacking proper insulation. I did my best to hold in the warmth with thick curtains and blinds. Without the heater, however, the apartment became bitterly cold.

I called the landlord, who said he would send a serviceman out the following day. He didn't want to pay an extra charge for someone to come after hours. I was very frustrated, but there was nothing I could do except to dress the kids warmly in many layers of clothing and to tuck them into bed with hats on their heads. I was up most of the night checking on all of them to make sure they were warm enough. I kept baby Jessica near me. The following day couldn't come soon enough. Thank God the furnace was repaired, and the apartment began to heat up again.

Meanwhile the neighbors upstairs—a man, his girlfriend, and her two children—began acting up. The man was often drunk in the evenings, and many times late at night he would pound on the walls on his way up his stairway, cursing and threatening to kill me.

Sometimes I asked my single brother to stay with me and the children until things settled down upstairs. His presence was a real comfort. I called the police on many occasions, but by the time they arrived the man had quieted down and so he didn't get caught. Finally one night the police caught him in action and arrested him. Then I had to be concerned that he might try to get revenge. Such was life in a cheap apartment building.

Christmas was just around the corner. I didn't have an extra dime to buy the children gifts, but I did make a few presents. A couple of weeks before Christmas the doorbell rang. Opening the door, I saw a pretty Christmas tree leaning against the porch and two people waving and smiling as they got into their truck. "Merry Christmas!" they shouted, and off they went.

We were just gifted a Christmas tree! I was thrilled that we would have this holiday tradition to brighten our humble abode. I put it up in front of the bay window in the living room. It was tall, nearly touching the ceiling. The kids and I decorated the tree as we sang a few Christmas carols. That night the glow of the colored lights strung through the branches gave the room an aura of hope.

I received a few gifts from our parish and secretly sneaked them into the house. The church also promised a turkey or a ham and a few other food items for our Christmas dinner. On Christmas Eve, the children and I said our prayers together, and then Chaldea placed a birthday card to Jesus under the tree.

After everyone was tucked into bed, I sat in the quiet living room alone, praying a few last prayers before getting ready to retire for the night. When I knew the children were fast asleep, I quietly placed Santa's gifts under the tree. At about nine o'clock I heard a soft tapping on the front door. I wasn't sure if I should answer the door but decided I would. It turned out to be a couple I knew who had taken it upon themselves to collect some gifts for the kids. The presents were all lovingly wrapped and tagged. Overwhelmed by their generosity, I was speechless. When I could finally say something, I expressed my thanks with tears of joy. I sensed that by accepting their marvelous gesture I was also giving a gift to them, since my joy completed their wonderful act of kindness.

The kids were very happy the following morning when they opened their gifts. Some of the tags said that elves had helped to wrap them! We then went off to our parish for Mass to celebrate Jesus' birthday. After our Christmas dinner we enjoyed a piece of birthday cake in Jesus' honor.

Mother Mary Gives Me Peace

I decided to take a mini-pilgrimage to the Shrine of Our Lady of Czestochowa, Queen of Peace, in Doylestown, Pennsylvania. It was certainly a lot closer to Connecticut and easier to get to than the shrine in Poland where the miraculous image of the Blessed Mother is especially known and venerated. It would have been impossible for me to escape to Poland in any case. But I was seeking peace. My heart was troubled by the realization that my marriage to Chris was going to end in divorce.

Our Lady of Czestochowa, also known as the Black Madonna, was beloved by Saint John Paul II, who made countless visits to Czestochowa, Poland, to venerate the image there. Prior to becoming pope, he had made two separate visits to the shrine in Doylestown, and in 1980 as pope he blessed the copy of the image that hangs in the lower church.

Our Lady of Czestochowa has an amazing history. Tradition holds that the image was created by Saint Luke the Evangelist, who is said to have painted Mary and the Christ Child on a wooden table made by Saint Joseph. The image was discovered by Saint Helena early in the fourth century, and many miracles have been attributed to it over the centuries.

Prayer and reflection before this miraculous image have indeed brought a good deal of peace to my heart. A small picture of the Black Madonna that once belonged to my grandmother hangs in my home.

Pope Francis said,

> Mary is so closely united to Jesus because she received from Him the knowledge of the heart, the knowledge of faith, nourished by her experience as a mother and by her close relationship with her Son. The Blessed Virgin is the woman of faith who made room for God in her heart and in her plans; she is the believer capable of perceiving in the gift of her Son the coming of that 'fullness of time' (Gal 4:4) in which God, by choosing the humble path of human existence, entered personally into the history of salvation. That is why Jesus cannot be understood without His Mother.
>
> (Homily, January 1, 2015)

Eventually after much prayer, spiritual counseling, and reflection, I knew I had to move forward and file for a divorce. It was a tough decision because I didn't want to let go of hope, but I did feel at peace. Chris didn't show up at the courthouse for the divorce. It was yet another challenging moment for me to get through on my own. Despite how I felt, I knew deep inside that I was not alone.

Shortly after the divorce, I got word from one of Chris' relatives that she wanted the cross that she had given to my daughter Chaldea at her Baptism. I sadly returned it, and Chris' family chose to cease contact afterward. Little did I know that I would see that cross again.

With the divorce behind me, I filed for an annulment at the encouragement of my spiritual director. The process was an interesting and sometimes challenging journey, but I felt it was a healing one and even necessary. The Church granted a decree of nullity, meaning that a sacramental marital bond between me and Chris had never taken place.

Surprise!

There was a knock at the door one afternoon. I answered it to find a woman from the welfare department who said she had come to search my apartment. *Search my apartment? What the heck is going on?* I wondered. As I had predicted when I applied for assistance, I was being subjected to government scrutiny. I guess I hadn't expected to feel violated in my own home though. The woman explained that someone had told the welfare department that a man was living with me. If she could prove that was the case, she said, my benefits would be terminated immediately.

I let the woman in and told her that my brother sometimes stayed overnight on my couch when I was frightened by the crazy neighbors upstairs. She disregarded what I was saying as she meandered through my living room, and I could feel my blood starting to boil. *Why should I be subjected to this nonsense?* I thought. *I didn't do anything wrong. This is ridiculous!*

"You see that picture there?" I asked her as I pointed to the image of the Sacred Heart of Jesus that hung in a prominent place in my living room. "THAT is the man I am living with!" She seemed unmoved by my bold proclamation, and she continued to snoop around until I finally told her that I wished she would leave so that Jessica's nap wouldn't be interrupted. She had seen enough, she said, and left. I was notified later that the state was satisfied with my participation in their program and that my benefits would continue.

There was never a dull moment in that place. On several nights when I was getting the children settled for bed, the upstairs neighbors dropped bowling balls on their floor—our ceiling—to disturb us. Once as I stepped onto the front porch of the apartment, one of the teenagers from upstairs rode his skateboard right over my foot, fracturing a few little bones on the top. He didn't even apologize.

My friend and spiritual director, Father Bill, suggested that I pray to Saint Joseph for help with my housing situation. I chose to pray a thirty-day novena. On the thirtieth day I heard a truck engine outside my apartment. I peered outside my window and was thrilled to observe a moving truck being loaded up with my upstairs neighbors' belongings. They were moving out! What an amazing answer to prayer and the beginning of my friendship with dear Saint Joseph. I began to understand why Saint Teresa of Avila had said that he never failed her.

8

Guided to a Saint: Mother Teresa in My Life

Jesus is pleased to come to us as the truth to be told and the life to be lived, as the light to be lighted and the love to be loved, as the joy to be given and the peace to be spread.

—Blessed Mother Teresa

Little Jessica was growing by leaps and bounds. Justin and Chaldea showered her with lots of love. We thoroughly enjoyed playing board games together, going for walks, playing outside, and in warmer weather planting flowers and vegetables in the yard.

As difficult as it was raising a family alone, I was extremely thankful for the gift of my children. I knew deep in my heart that God was with us in our little domestic church. He gave me the strength to put one foot in front of the other each day to walk in faith. I felt a profound need to raise my children with a solid foundation of faith, and I am very thankful that I possessed the wherewithal to continue in the right direction spiritually. Though striving for holiness, we didn't on any given day resemble a page in *Butler's Lives of the Saints*—maybe far from it! We certainly didn't have sparkling halos hovering over our heads. Rather, we were a work in progress as we moved forward in faith.

Every day as a single mother meant being in survival mode. In the winter, for example, I learned how to restart my furnace with kerosene when I ran out of the more expensive heating oil. Many nights our dinners consisted of tomato soup and grilled cheese sandwiches or something similar, courtesy of the local soup kitchen located near our apartment. I used to stop over there at a specific time of day a few days a week to pick up a goody bag that the kind volunteers had packed for us. At times, if the children were sick and I couldn't get out, I would give the soup kitchen a call and they would have someone drop off the meal to me. Not many people knew about this because it was quite awkward to let on that we ate from a soup kitchen. I didn't tell the children because I wanted to prevent them embarrassment. I tried to keep home life as normal and natural as possible, all the while teaching the children to count their blessings and to give generously to others.

Speaking of giving generously to others, one time on my birthday, which is in late November, the children made sweet homemade cards and baked me a cake! We enjoyed a simple celebration together. Later that evening when I went into my bedroom to get ready for bed, I found an envelope on my bureau. "Mom" was written on the outside. I opened it up to find one hundred dollars in tens and twenties! There was a little note inside from my daughter Chaldea, telling me that I should use the money to buy Christmas presents. She selflessly gave me all of her hard-earned babysitting money so that I could provide presents under our Christmas tree, and she didn't want any credit herself. I cried a few quiet tears of joy and gratitude and then went to my daughter to thank and hug her. My heart was bursting with the mother's pride I felt for my thoughtful and generous daughter.

A Dream Come True?

Little Jessica was now almost two years old. My neighbors told me about a marriageable bachelor they knew named Charlie (not his real name). It was obvious they were trying to play matchmaker, and I politely told them that I didn't want to take part. They kept it up on both ends for some time. I later heard that they told Charlie I was an "angel"; they told me he went to daily Mass. That, I admit, was a bit intriguing. *He goes to daily Mass—really? Does he also have a white horse?* My neighbors told me he was a practicing attorney and drove a nice car. They seemed to think that Charlie's financial situation might be appealing to me.

When Charlie's dog had a litter of ten puppies that were just about ready to be given away, I agreed to meet the puppies and to consider getting one for the kids. It was all arranged, and I went over to meet Charlie and his puppies, finding the latter to be cute and rambunctious. I should have had my head examined though, because I agreed to take a puppy home for the kids. It would be another mouth to feed.

The little visit with Charlie and the puppies went well, and Charlie asked me out to dinner. We seemed to hit it off and started to spend a lot of time together. Before long Charlie asked me to marry him. We had seen each other so often that it seemed like much more time had gone by than really had. About six months after we met we were married.

One night during our engagement, I slid my engagement ring off my finger and set it on my night stand. I was feeling uneasy about Charlie, and at that moment I didn't know if I would ever put the ring back on. My concerns were smoothed over though, and I was again wearing my ring before Charlie ever knew I had taken it off. The night before our wedding, however, I became really scared. I wondered if I should call off the wedding. A few things about his personality seemed to raise red flags, and I called a priest friend to share my fears. He listened to my concerns and then brushed them away. "The love will see you through," he said. Since I trusted God with my life and sought advice from a priest I considered very wise, I chose to believe his words.

We got married in the Church and moved to a picturesque little town. We settled into a small house set back on a hill overlooking pretty meadows dotted with grazing sheep. It was a short walk or drive to the village store, the post office, the library, and a playground. We enrolled the children in a nearby Catholic school and began to enjoy a kind of family life that the kids and I hadn't experienced in a long while—a two-parent home.

Trouble in Paradise

I started realizing things about our relationship that troubled me. At times I felt as though Charlie were grilling me with questions, and I thought maybe he behaved in this confrontational way because he was an attorney. Our difficulties, however, proved to be more than differences in temperament. Often Charlie would say, "I couldn't disagree with you more." We seldom seemed to be on the same page.

My biggest problem, however, was that Charlie seemed to be jealous of the children. For instance, if one of them cried, especially Jessica, he said it was a demon in the child. This response was very disconcerting, so I questioned him about it; but he did not give me a straight answer. He also didn't like it when I tended to an important need of one of the children, and he had to wait a moment for me to come back to him. I surmised that maybe having been single without the responsibilities of children coupled with being the head of a law office had made him accustomed to having his needs met in a more timely fashion. Also troubling were some of Charlie's religious practices. For example, when we traveled, he would place a piece of silk cloth on his seat because he didn't want to get someone else's karma.

I figured that we would have to adapt to one another and prayerfully make adjustments and compromises. I knew there would be some give and take, as there is in every marriage, but I was also keenly aware that I would not be able to tolerate anything harmful to me or the children.

Charlie began to open up little by little about a religious group he had been part of in another country prior to meeting me. He had had a leadership role and had answered to a guru with whom he had been involved for about ten years. I tried to understand what he had gone through by listening carefully and then putting together bits and pieces of what he said with what I would discover later on through some digging. But whenever I inquired about the group, even very gently, Charlie became very defensive and lashed out or shut down completely. It was a waiting game. I had to wait until he revealed the things he wanted me to know.

One time when I tried to talk with him about the group, Charlie got very angry. He became brusque and then started to yell at me, so I got up from the kitchen table and started walking toward the dishwasher, which was open. I shut the door as I walked by, and the next thing I knew, my shoulders were being painfully yanked backwards. Charlie had grabbed me from behind and was yelling at me. "That's violent!" he shouted, accusing me of violently slamming the dishwasher door. I hadn't slammed the door. I had simply closed it because it was open and in the way. But that is not how Charlie had interpreted my behavior. As he continued to shout at me, I became so frightened that I ran to the bedroom and locked myself in. He kicked in the door, and I ran to the phone to call my spiritual director to seek prayers and advice. Charlie grabbed the phone out of my hands and pulled the cord out of the wall. He clearly did not want anyone to know what was going on.

Days later I went to a massage therapist for my sore neck and shoulders. He knew Charlie, and I asked him if he knew whether Charlie had acted violently before. He told me that Charlie had done something similar to his ex-wife, and I begged him not to let Charlie know that we had discussed the incident. I was devastated that my husband had physically abused me.

The Cult

From what I was observing of Charlie's behaviors and beliefs, I suspected that he had been part of a strange cult and that he was still emotionally and spiritually attached to it. He sometimes became very down on himself. His mood would plummet after he listened to audio tapes about Transcendental Meditation (TM) and messages from the cult leader Ronald (not his real name), who had created these tapes to maintain control over his followers even from afar. Ronald's group was a spin-off of the TM movement and incorporated ideas from Erhard Seminars Training (EST). In his writings, the cult leader said he experienced a conviction that he should turn to Catholic tradition while still retaining all of the Eastern and Hindu practices he had adopted.

Charlie admitted that he was involved in TM, an ancient meditation technique dusted off by Maharishi Mahesh Yogi. TM might seem innocent and perhaps even helpful, and it was touted as beneficial by some in the medical field. But a myriad of serious, harmful side effects have been connected with the practice, including chronic dissociation from reality, which is probably the most dangerous. Other problems associated with TM include difficulty coming out of the trance induced by the practice, mental breakdowns and disorders, anxiety, and suicidal tendencies.

Some users swear by the technique, but using TM is deliberately putting oneself into a trance. Practitioners do this by reciting a particular mantra, which is a kind of prayer to a Hindu god. Ultimately, reciting the mantra invites spiritual entities into a person's life intentionally or not. As I found this out, I knew at the deepest part of my being that Charlie was in trouble. We were in trouble.

Once when Charlie was walking through the yard listening to a cassette tape through headphones, he stopped suddenly and pulled off the headphones. He yanked the cassette tape out of the player and threw it against some rocks. His getting upset was a good sign. It seemed he was trying to break free from the control that the cult had on him. But before long guilt and despair took over.

When Charlie was at work I rummaged through some cardboard boxes I discovered in our closet. There were numerous letters from Ronald, the cult leader, lots of articles, and videotapes of some of the meetings. The letters made my hair stand on end. The guy was nuts! And vulnerable, unsuspecting people believed in him.

I pored over the newly discovered material for hours. Leaving papers scattered all over the floor, I got up from where I had been sitting and slid one of the tapes into our video player. After a few minutes of viewing the outlandish and perplexing tapes, my jaw must have literally dropped. I was shocked at what I saw and became extremely concerned for my husband and my marriage too. The problem was much bigger than the practice of TM. These videos showed a crazy individual who publicly humiliated people in the name of some cosmic cause, some kind of nutty enlightenment. I could see why Charlie despaired so when he listened to the tapes. The criticism drew him back into the pit. My husband had been one of the victims of verbal abuse in front of the group. The leader had destroyed a part of Charlie. The damage done was serious.

I put all of the stuff back into the boxes and shoved them into the closet. Then I got right down on my knees and prayed. *Dear Lord, please help me to help my husband.* What was I to do? After praying, I picked up the phone and made some calls. Soon I was speaking with the secretary of the prominent theologian Father John A. Hardon, S.J. She put me in touch with the world-renowned Jesuit scholar, who is now deceased and whose cause for canonization has been opened. I found out that Father Hardon had been counseling people who had been part of this peculiar cult. It seemed bizarre, yet providential to be in touch with Father Hardon at that critical time, when he was intensely involved in helping people to get out of the cult safely. I had no doubt whatsoever that God had his hand in all of it. He was helping me to get help for my husband.

I told Father Hardon about my husband's behavior, the videotapes, and the letters. He was extraordinarily understanding. He knew all about the cult leader and his tactics as well as the deep and severe harm that he had inflicted upon his followers. Father Hardon's calm words were reassuring even though I was quite frightened about my situation. Father invited me, along with Charlie and the children, to visit him in Washington, D.C. I accepted his kind invitation, feeling confident that God would use him to help Charlie. I asked Father to pray that I could work it out so that we would be able to go. I knew in my heart that if it was meant to be, we would meet Father Hardon, but I also knew that I needed to proceed prudently.

By the grace of God and Father Hardon's prayers, I was able to persuade Charlie that we should set a date to meet the priest. It had to be a miracle that Charlie agreed to go because he was normally very resistant. Washington, D.C., was about an eight-hour ride from where we lived in Connecticut, and it wouldn't be exactly easy to pull off the trip with three kids along.

One night before we left for Washington, Charlie became distraught. He said he felt as if thousands of demons were attacking him. They were crawling all over his face and sticking him with what felt like sharp pins and needles all over his body. His distress thoroughly upset me. I prayed quietly and tried to reassure him. I could not wait to get on the road to see Father Hardon.

We finally set out on our trip. We planned to visit Charlie's friends who were once a part of the cult and lived about halfway to our destination. We had a meal with them, and before we parted his friend handed me a magazine article about the cult. I folded it up and quickly put it in my purse. Charlie had noticed what had transpired and quickly ushered the children and me out of his friends' home and into our car to get back on the road.

Not more than a half mile down the road, Charlie suddenly pulled the car over to the side of the highway. He leaned over and got right in my face. "Where's that article?" he asked, clenching his teeth and sounding as if he were going to take my head off. He was extremely agitated.

He immediately got out of the car, opened the trunk, and flung all the suitcases onto the ground, right there on the side of the road. Ranting and raving, he opened every suitcase and emptied the contents. His outburst was extremely unsettling; I was worried about the children and any passersby seeing him in that insane rage. I just wanted to get to Father Hardon safely so that Charlie could be helped somehow. It seemed that the meeting was in danger of being sabotaged and that perhaps "you-know-who" (as I call the evil one) was not happy.

I quickly reached into my purse and handed Charlie the article. Then I scooped up all of our stuff and crammed it back into the suitcases. We got back on the road in silence. Without a sound, I prayed the Rosary for the remainder of the trip, discreetly moving the beads through my fingers, pausing every so often to speak to the children in the back seat when they needed something.

Struck by Holiness

We arrived safely at our hotel and somehow got to sleep that night. Charlie had cooled down. The next morning we met Father Hardon at his residence. He greeted us with a warm smile and almost inaudible words. He was small in stature and slightly frail-looking with white hair and penetrating eyes. He wore a long black cassock that swept the floor; he seemed to float when he walked. He escorted us to a quiet area where we could talk. As we conversed, his warmth and humility were very perceptible, as well as the depth of his wisdom. He was known in many circles for his holiness and his loyalty to the Magisterium of the Church. Many believed him to be a living saint.

Father Hardon's words that morning snapped Charlie right out of the cult. Just like that! It was quite remarkable. Charlie was thankful and seemed instantly transformed. I hoped that things would continue to get better and that our marriage would grow stronger.

After our meeting with Father Hardon, I stayed in touch with him for many years. We spoke a lot by telephone, and we used snail mail because email was not yet invented. I was blessed to attend a few of his women's retreats and Marian Catechist retreats. Father became my spiritual director and, later on, my daughter's godfather.

Over the next several months we invited various cult members to our home. They stayed with us for a few days or weeks as we helped them to realize the dangers of the cult and offered our support. One person who came to visit for a few weeks was the cult leader's wife. She had perhaps been the most abused. All of the former cult members who stayed with us suffered terribly from low self-esteem. They had been psychologically and emotionally abused not only by the cult leader but also by fellow cult members who had been instructed to take certain actions against them.

One Saint Leads Me to Another

During our meeting with Father Hardon, he told us about the Missionaries of Charity (the order founded by Mother Teresa) located in a poor section of Washington, D.C. He was one of Mother Teresa's spiritual directors and gave retreats to the sisters. He encouraged us to make time to visit them, and to visit the sick and dying who were staying in the Gift of Peace House, which was part of their convent. From my earlier conversations with Father Hardon, he knew that I liked to take the children on visits to hospitals and nursing homes, training them in works of mercy.

Since Father Hardon thought it was a good idea, we mustered up the confidence to make the trip to the convent. The sisters greeted us warmly with big, contagious smiles. They showed us around and brought us to see the sick and dying. It quickly became apparent to me why the sick, in spite of their suffering, seemed to have a deep peace about them. They were being cared for by angels! The joy the sisters radiated and the love that flowed from them gave a much-needed dose of hope and peace to all around them.

After we finished visiting the patients, the sisters invited us to come back the following day to one of their private Masses. There would be two Masses, and Mother Teresa would be at one of them. *What?* Yes, I heard correctly. Mother Teresa of Calcutta would be at one of the Masses the following day.

We decided to get up very early. Well, 5:00 A.M. is pretty early to rouse sleepy children who want to hug their warm pillows a little longer. But the children knew we were doing something special. Since we were going to see the sisters again, they didn't complain too much.

We arrived at the convent a little before 7:00 A.M., in time for Mass. We noticed that many pairs of sandals and a few pairs of shoes were lined up outside the door to the chapel. So we slipped our shoes off too, and placed them alongside the others. Then we tiptoed inside.

I couldn't help but see many saints in the making as I peered at the numerous sisters who filled the chapel, all kneeling down, heads bowed in prayer—they looked like a sea of white saris trimmed in blue.

The next thing I noticed, straight across the room, was something painted on the wall next to the tabernacle: the words "I Thirst." Mother Teresa wanted everyone who entered any one of the Missionaries of Charity chapels in various parts of the world to see those words, to ponder Jesus' great thirst for our love, and further, to consider that we should thirst for Him as well.

I found an open spot on the floor and knelt down with the children and Charlie. I wanted to blend in. But was that even possible? I'm sure we were very noticeable, especially when my littlest, Jessica, not quite two years old, decided to express her needs. Her little (and not so little!) sounds necessitated several trips outside so as not to disturb anyone during Mass.

The very next thing that caught my eye was actually the lack of things. The chapel had none of the creature comforts to which we are accustomed, nor even the common items one normally encounters in a chapel. There were no stained glass windows, carpeting, heat or air conditioning, nor any pews or chairs. It was very stark and simple, which created an atmosphere of peace and holiness.

Mother Teresa taught her sisters to live as the poor. She wanted them to understand fully their plight so that they could love them properly. Genuine peace of soul comes from not being attached to material things. Mother Teresa wanted that for her sisters, priests, and brothers.

Mass was about to begin. My eyes were partially closed as I quietly prayed and watched over the kids. Suddenly I sensed an arresting holy presence beside me on my left. I can't describe it. I cracked open my eyes to discover Mother Teresa walking right past me—her bare feet making feather-light sounds on the floor until she knelt down and blended in with the sisters.

Mass was truly beautiful, though I missed bits and pieces of it as I traipsed in and out as quietly as possible with a toddler in tow.

Meeting the Saint of the Gutters

Directly after Mass, before exiting the chapel and making our way into the convent's foyer, we bid our good-bye to Jesus in the Blessed Sacrament hidden in the tabernacle. Six-year-old Chaldea sweetly genuflected, and the next thing I knew, a kindhearted nun ran up behind her to give her a big squeezing hug. She then went into a room with the other sisters.

Wow, these sisters are so caring and sweet, I mused.

Before I could even finish my thought, I realized that the kind nun was none other than Mother Teresa!

We stood in a little huddle out in the foyer trying to comprehend our blessings. We knew that it was very special just to be in the same room with someone whom we—and most of the world—considered to be a living saint. My heart was singing because Mother Teresa had given my daughter a hug!

After a few minutes the door across the room opened and there she was again. Mother Teresa, the saint of the gutters, was walking straight toward me! By this time I had Jessica secure in my arms so that she couldn't run around. As Mother Teresa approached, I had no time to worry about what I would do or say when face to face with her. She reached out her worn, wrinkled hand to touch Jessica, and I would later ponder about how the same hand that lovingly cared for the poorest of the poor—extracting maggots, bathing, caressing, baptizing, consoling, and much more—had also touched my family. Mother Teresa took the time to reach out to ordinary people.

Then she asked me, "Is this the baby who was singing at Mass?" How delightful that she referred to a fussy baby as a "singing" baby! We all smiled, and Mother Teresa proceeded to hand each of us a blessed Miraculous Medal that she had first kissed. We accepted her gifts, and our conversation with her began. I had no idea then about how Mother Teresa's gift of the Miraculous Medal would impact my life, but more on that later. Mother Teresa told me that my children were very fortunate to have a family. She was much more accustomed to devastating poverty and picking up abandoned children and babies from dustbins. I told Mother Teresa that I agreed—I felt truly blessed to have my children.

While we were talking, Jessica wanted to get down from my arms. Mother Teresa motioned for the child to come to her, and Jessica, who was usually very shy with strangers, didn't hesitate for a second when Mother Teresa beckoned. As they stood together, holding hands, Jessica peered up into Mother Teresa's eyes, and the whole room fell silent as everyone present observed the intensity and duration of the child's look. Mother Teresa remarked that Jessica might become a Missionary of Charity one day.

After a while, I knew that we should let Mother Teresa return to her duties. She no doubt had important work to do, and I didn't want to keep her from it. The kids all gave her a warm hug good-bye. I did, as well. I felt as though I was hugging a relative, someone I had known all my life. In that time we shared together our hearts became intertwined somehow.

As she left the room, Mother Teresa turned around once more to ask us to pray for her and to pray for the poor. We promised our prayers.

A lay coworker present that day had snapped a few photos of our encounter with Mother Teresa. Before we left she asked for our address and offered to lend us the negatives (in the days before digital cameras) to print into photos. Some of the photos have been published in my book *Mother Teresa and Me: Ten Years of Friendship*.

I later learned that Mother Teresa was not fond of having her picture taken. So much did she dislike it that she considered it a form of penance. She said she made a deal with God that for each photo that was snapped of her God should release a soul from purgatory.

Back to Reality?

All the way home to Connecticut I thought about our amazing encounter with holiness and jotted down a few notes. I pondered and I prayed. Life would never be the same. How could it be after meeting such living saints as Father Hardon and Mother Teresa? I also thanked God for his great mercy in helping Charlie, through Father Hardon.

I wanted to send Mother Teresa a note of thanks to show my appreciation for her time and the blessed medals. The thought continued to prod me, but each time I dismissed it because I knew full well that Mother Teresa was a busy woman. She was chosen by God to serve the poorest of the poor all over the world and teach the world about love. She had already given us enough of her valuable time so I shouldn't take more from her by writing her a note she would have to read, I told myself. Yet, the thought wouldn't leave me alone, so I decided I would consult with the mother superior of the convent we visited. She would know what to do.

I called her on the phone and asked for her advice.

"Yes, Donna, you should write to her," she reassured me.

"Are you sure, Mother Dolores?" I wanted to be absolutely certain. The last thing I wanted was to distract Mother Teresa with silly things.

"Yes! Here's her address ..."

I took her eagerness as a message from God: I should write to Mother Teresa. I poured out my heart in a handwritten letter and mailed it to Calcutta, and a few weeks later I received a reply from Mother Teresa.

I'll never forget pulling it out of the mailbox and seeing the Calcutta, India, return address in the corner of the envelope. I carefully took out the letter, typed on thin paper, and unfolded it slowly. As I read, my heart rejoiced to realize the care with which Mother had chosen her words. Later I heard from some sisters that she had composed the letter on an old typewriter late at night. With so many other duties, she nevertheless had taken the time to write me back.

As amazed as I was to receive a letter from a living saint, I actually thought of Mother Teresa as a friend, a mentor, and a mother figure. Her head wasn't in the clouds as one might suppose. She was extremely down to earth and totally in touch with the practical needs of the day. She was no stranger to the realities of modern life and therefore was able to counsel people in a prudent and appropriate manner, all the while being in touch with the spiritual side of things too. I don't know how many times I read that letter from Mother Teresa. But each time I discovered new meaning in her profound words. I was being guided by a saint!

Over the years I would be privileged to receive many more letters from that humble woman. There were twenty-two to be exact. In God's divine providence I was further blessed with many more visits with Mother Teresa, as well. There were more than a dozen, and some of them were private. I could never have imagined all of this would come to pass during my first conversation with Mother in Washington, D.C. I am very thankful I carried out the deep inspiration I felt to send that first letter to Mother Teresa.

What did I do with all of those blessings? At first I kept them quiet. I didn't want to sound as if I were bragging that I knew two saints: Father Hardon and Mother Teresa. But years later, it became necessary for the blessings to come out in the open.

After meeting Mother Teresa and spending time with her sisters in their New York convents, I did a lot of pondering and praying about what God might be calling me to do. I had previously become a member of the Third Order of Saint Dominic in an attempt to grow in holiness, but I began to be drawn to Mother Teresa's spirituality. In time I sought and received permission from the Dominicans to leave their order so that I could become a member of the Lay Missionaries of Charity. The sisters and some other lay members encouraged me to open a branch of the group in my area, and I did.

Rickety Beds and Feasts from Garbage

Father Hardon told me that he was going to give a weekend retreat to the sisters in Harlem, New York. Mother Teresa would be there, and

Father invited me to partake of the retreat and the spiritual life of the sisters. I was a married woman with three children, but I was going to spend a weekend at a convent! If that wasn't ironic enough, I would be staying in the women's homeless shelter run by the sisters.

At the shelter attached to their convent in Harlem, I slept on a rickety metal bunk bed in a room full of women from all sorts of backgrounds. They all seemed pretty grateful to be there. I was too, but I was accustomed to my own comfy bed at home in the quiet rural town where I lived. That weekend was a bit challenging for me because I didn't get much sleep; I wasn't used to hearing many people tossing and turning on squeaky beds and snoring the night away while sirens and boom boxes blared outside in the streets. I didn't wake up very refreshed in the mornings, and my head pounded with migraines. But the experience was good for me and perhaps helped me to understand the plight of the poor a bit better.

At that time, in 1988, Harlem was a dangerous area. Barbed wire seemed to be the decoration of choice. Old beat-up cars without engines lined the street, and graffiti and garbage were everywhere. When I arrived at the convent, I clutched my rosary beads tightly in one hand and pounded on the door of the shelter with the other. I prayed that I could get inside safely because I had observed shady-looking characters nearby. Eventually, the huge door creaked open and I slipped inside.

The sisters welcomed me with smiling faces and showed me to a room where they offered me a cup of tea and a bite to eat. A little later Father Hardon found me and said, "Make sure you roll up your sleeves." It was his polite way of telling me to help the sisters while there. I learned early on that Father Hardon was a diligent worker in the Lord's vineyard. He had a catch phrase: "There's work to be done!" He regularly reminded the people around him that our Lord was counting on them.

Each morning the women from the shelter and I sorted through, washed, and prepared fruits and vegetables that would be used later for meals. Most of the food was donated by the local grocery stores. It was usually expired or slightly bruised or rotten. The sisters were happy to receive their throwaways and combined the best bits and pieces with love to make tasty and nourishing meals for the homeless they served in their soup kitchen.

While sorting through the fruits and vegetables, I tossed out a rotten pear. Just then a sister was walking by. She stopped, peered into the trash can, and retrieved the pear I had thrown away. As she handed it to me, she pointed out the one salvageable spot on the rotten fruit and then walked on—as simple as that. The experience taught me an important lesson: every good little bit was important and worth saving. I don't think I ever looked at a piece of rotten or bruised food the same way again. From then on I tried my very best never to waste food.

In the early evenings, we manned our stations in the kitchen and got ready for the massive groups of people who would hurriedly come through the doors to dine. Some were sworn enemies, yet for a time they would be together in the same room by God's grace and the work of the sisters. I was told to heap food on the plates since the meal might be their only one for a while.

My eyes met those of the guests a few times as I handed them their plates of hot food. It was an experience I can't describe. Mother Teresa was indeed rubbing off on me. I began to see Jesus in those I served. Mother Teresa wholeheartedly lived by Matthew 25:40: "Truly, I say to you, as you did it to one of the least of these my brethren, you did it to me." To teach this essential message, Mother would often hold up her hand and as she bent down each finger she would say, "You—did—it—to—me!" Whatever we do or don't do to others, we do or don't do to Him. Those simple yet poignant words give us much to think about. How do we treat Jesus in others?

United in Prayer with Mother Teresa

I felt blessed whenever I prayed with the sisters during the weekend. Those few moments I was able to slip into the chapel by myself, to spend a little time with Jesus in the Blessed Sacrament, were blessings too. Once when I was in the chapel alone, Mother Teresa came in. She glanced at me then knelt on the bare floor, folded her hands, and bowed her head. I'll never forget that image of her or the feeling of being united with her in prayer. Mother Teresa said, "Love is the reason for my life." God was calling me to a life of love too, as He calls all of us.

The sisters were called to prayer by the ringing of a bell. I would hear the distinct sound of the bell numerous times over the days I spent with the sisters. I was also summoned to prayer by the bell—very different from the one earlier in my life, but nonetheless, it beckoned me. Later on, I would reflect on how a mother's "bell" or call to active and prayerful service is the sound of her baby crying for food or her family needing her in some way. The "bell" to pray also rings within the vocation of motherhood. Mothers have to try their best to be attentive to it.

Soon after I returned home from the Harlem convent I learned that I was expecting a baby. What a joy for me to realize that my little unborn baby had also been reaping the benefits of being with the sisters, Mother Teresa, and Father Hardon.

I began to experience some trouble with my heart and was required to take daily medication. My heart raced uncontrollably without it, and I was told that the medication would be safe for my baby.

In the spring, Father Hardon entrusted Charlie and me with a little mission. He asked us to hand-deliver some of his papers about his developing Marian Catechists to the president of the Pontifical Council for the Laity, Eduardo Cardinal Pironio. Charlie and I were blessed to take the trip to Rome, where we had a very nice meeting with the cardinal. Later, I received a beautiful letter from him with a blessing for us and the baby we were expecting.

While in Rome we attended one of Pope John Paul II's general audiences and toured around a bit. I was ill with a bladder infection the whole trip and began running a fever. We stayed with the sweet Polish nuns who lived near the Vatican, and they were very kind to me, knowing that I was pregnant and not feeling well. The trip was short and extremely meaningful, but I was happy to get home to the children.

Later on in the pregnancy I became sick again with a high fever, and this time I also had a bad cough. When the fever wouldn't break after three days, even though I was on a fever reducer, I called the doctor. He told me to go to the hospital when my husband got home so that I could be checked for pneumonia. I asked if I could hold off and see if the fever would go away that night. He warned me that having a fever for so long was creating a dangerous environment for the baby.

When Charlie came home I told him that I needed to go to the hospital.

"What did you do?" he asked. He reacted angrily, saying he was supposed to give a presentation that night. I told him not to worry, that I would get myself to the hospital, and he calmed down and drove me there.

I recovered from the illness, and my pregnancy progressed nicely. The Missionaries of Charity sisters were praying for me and the baby, and during another visit with Mother Teresa at their convent in New York, she placed her hand on my abdomen and blessed my unborn baby.

Looking forward to the birth, I was eager to turn a tiny room off our bedroom into a nursery. That had been our plan all along. There was a desk in there that Charlie sometimes used, and after I hung the border on the wall and added the crib and the small dresser, Charlie reprimanded me for destroying his office. I felt sad, because it seemed as though he cared more about keeping the desk than about making room for the baby.

Shortly before the birth, Charlie and I disagreed about something else. He became so angry that he lunged toward me as he yelled at me and tried to grab me. Although nine months pregnant, I eluded his grasp and ran upstairs to the bedroom, where I began to telephone Father Bill. Charlie pushed in the door and yanked the phone out of my hands. Once again he pulled the cord out of the wall.

After the incident was over, I kept my distance from Charlie so that he could calm down. The next day he brought me some kind of gift. I don't remember now what it was. Sometimes after his rages he would bring me flowers. Sometimes he would apologize and renew his affection for me and the children. But sometimes, instead of apologizing, he would say that what had happened was my fault or wasn't as bad as I said it was and that I was exaggerating.

In time I learned from a counselor that this way of expressing remorse or of shifting blame is a manipulative tool used by abusive people in an attempt to absolve themselves of responsibility. Abusers use a variety of tactics to maintain power and control, and unfortunately the cycle of abuse goes round and round. Discussing this with the counselor helped me to understand Charlie's changes in mood and behavior. Suddenly everything came into focus for me, as when I put on my first pair of eyeglasses. But, even so, my trust in Charlie was wearing thin.

I confided my marriage troubles to Mother Teresa, who assured me that she prayed many prayers for me. Here is a quote from one of her letters:

> I am sorry to hear about your trials. I am praying for [Charlie] that he may come to realize that he too has been created for greater things—to love and be loved. The most trying behavior is only a cry for love, for acceptance—for healing. Allow that healing to come to [him] through you—his own family, by loving him with tender, understanding love.

Pray together as a family, for the family that prays together, stays together in love, peace, and unity. I know it is not always easy to love. But when you love till it hurts—there is no more hurt—but only more love. I am praying for you, asking Our Lady to be a Mother to you, to give you Her Heart so beautiful, so pure, so full of love and humility that you may receive Jesus in the Bread of Life and love and serve Him in the distressing disguise of your husband.

Mother Teresa's words sustained me throughout the inner turmoil I suffered in being married to a troubled man. With God's grace, I endeavored to continue to love Charlie even when it hurt to do so and to see him as "Jesus in the distressing disguise of the poorest of the poor".

Then unexpectedly, Charlie sought counseling. Unfortunately it did not seem that he was seeking help for himself, but only for me. He thought that I was not in touch with reality, that I had mental problems. I came to this conclusion from our numerous conversations, and it was confirmed years later when I found copies of his letters to the well-known psychiatrist in New York City he wanted us to see. In these letters Charlie wrote that I was crazy, and I later learned that deeply troubled people often project their problem onto another person, believing it is the other person who has the problem and not them. Projection is a coping mechanism.

I agreed to go to New York City to meet the doctor, who was Catholic. I was actually thrilled to go and very thankful to God that we might get some help. But after a few sessions, Charlie wanted us to stop going. Though we didn't benefit as a couple because Charlie didn't want to continue with the counseling, I felt comforted by the doctor's reassuring words to me about the state of my own mental health.

A New Baby in the House

It was time for our baby to be born. Little Joseph came into this world on a cold November morning. He was beautiful, and his older brother and sisters showered him with love. Mother Teresa and the sisters were very happy that he was born healthy and safely, knowing the health problems I had experienced during the pregnancy, which had necessitated the presence of a cardiologist at his cesarean birth.

Mother Teresa said, "I am happy for the gift of [the] baby boy that God has given you. He is a gift of God's love for you." Her words pierced my heart. "Keep the joy of loving Jesus in each other," she added. Mother Teresa was forever reminding me of God's precious gifts and of the importance of joy. She told her sisters that if they didn't possess joy in their hearts, they could pack up and go home. It might sound a bit harsh, but she was simply teaching the necessity of possessing joy and sharing it with the poor, who had enough troubles without encountering a grumpy nun.

When Joseph was only a few months old, the sisters let me know that Mother Teresa was back in the country. I called the convent and asked if I could stop by with little Joseph. (Perhaps it was funny to say "stop by" when I was more than a two-hour drive away.) I thought that Mother Teresa and the sisters might want to see a little baby that they had prayed for. And of course I wanted to take advantage of every chance the kids and I had to see Mother Teresa. I believed that rubbing elbows with holiness was a wonderful thing.

The children and I made the trip to the convent, where we were blessed with a private visit with Mother Teresa. She gently took Joseph out of my arms and held him up, rejoicing and thanking God. Mother looked into Joseph's eyes and tickled his chubby little legs. She raised him up a few times like a proud grandmother. Before we left, Mother Teresa gave me a wooden cross attached to a piece of a rawhide.

Joseph was a happy baby and grew into a happy little toddler. His older sister would dress him up in girl's clothes as if he were a doll. Joseph tolerated a lot and enjoyed all of the games.

Joseph and Jessica accompanied me to morning Mass at the chapel of the Catholic school their siblings attended. After Mass, the three of us spent some time adoring Jesus in the Blessed Sacrament. Jessica usually grew restless after a while and meandered out of the chapel and down the hallway to the classrooms. I didn't worry since the area was contained and there were no dangers. She often visited the older children and became a little mascot to the fourth graders.

Home life was pretty good in our charming little house in the countryside. The large windows provided a constant live movie of the nature right outside our doors. During happy times, the kids were content and played blissfully together. Little Joseph enjoyed singing songs and shooting balls into a child-sized basketball hoop. Justin enjoyed playing basketball on his school team, and Chaldea and Jessica were involved in continual creative adventures.

But we were enduring a good deal of strife. No one outside our home knew about the physical, emotional, and verbal abuse Charlie inflicted on me. To all unsuspecting onlookers we appeared to be the perfect family. I continued to pray for help in my marriage, and I was thankful to be grounded by Father Hardon's and Mother Teresa's prayers, teachings, and advice. I focused on raising the children.

In Honor of Saint Joseph

When Joseph was almost a year old, I felt inspired to open a small religious goods store. Charlie said he didn't see how I could operate it, let alone afford to open it. Sitting in our driveway was an old car I had driven before I married Charlie. He agreed that if I could sell the car, I could use the money to open up a little store. It would be up to me to work out the details, he said. I prayed to Saint Joseph and asked for his help. He must have interceded for me because the car sold almost immediately for $1,000, which I used to buy some inventory. I opened the store in an empty room across from Charlie's law office and paid Charlie rent, about $250 per month. I named my store Saint Joseph's Corner and invited my friend Father Bill to bless it prior to opening. The second floor wasn't exactly the ideal location, but interestingly the building was on Church Street, and people came from all areas of the state to shop there. Soon it became known as a place to find solid Catholic and other Christian books and religious articles that made nice gifts for First Communions and such. The place also developed a reputation for Catholic camaraderie, which was encouraged by a monthly spiritual newsletter that I published and mailed to my growing list of customers.

Recollecting one of the early orders I placed for the store brings a smile to my face now. By mistake I phoned in the wrong order number for a Saint Joseph statue. A two-and-a-half-foot statue was delivered instead of the six-inch model I thought I had ordered for a customer. I was going to return it, but instead, I paid for it and kept it to adorn my little shop named in Saint Joseph's honor. It seemed meant to be.

A few of my friends volunteered to help run the store, and later on my older children helped too. Whenever I was there my little ones were with me. I loved running Saint Joseph's Corner as an apostolate to provide spiritual nourishment and religious goods. There was no profit involved, though, and many times I found it difficult to pay the rent.

One of the rosaries from Saint Joseph's Corner became a spiritual link in a chain connecting me with Mother Teresa and John Cardinal O'Connor, the archbishop of New York. While on our way to New York City for a private event with Cardinal O'Conner, I felt inspired to stop at my store first. I ran in to grab my best rosary, hoping that, if it was meant to be, I would be able to give it to the cardinal. During the event, Cardinal O'Connor was making his way over to me and baby Joseph, who was sitting on my lap. I handed Joseph the rosary and told him to give the beads to the cardinal. When he gently received the rosary from Joseph, he looked pleasantly surprised and asked, "Why are you giving this to me?" I told him that I had felt inspired to do so. He said, "I just yesterday gave Mother Teresa my rosary because she told me that she had just given hers away." We both smiled, and I felt happy to be linked together to Mother Teresa through Mother Mary's rosary.

An Eventful Pregnancy

Life was extremely busy with four kids, and I often thought about my mother raising eight. But I thoroughly loved my vocation of motherhood despite the challenges. One day I discovered I was expecting another baby, and I was excited to know another precious child was on the way.

This was my eighth pregnancy. Four babies I had carried full term and three had gone to heaven through miscarriage. I felt delighted and blessed to have another child within me. My pregnancy started off fine, but then my heart problem started up again. The cardiologist put me on a triple dose of the medication I had taken during my pregnancy with Joseph, and my heart was monitored often.

When I was ten weeks pregnant, a disturbed woman from my parish stopped by one day when I was home alone. She let herself in the front door and came up the stairs to my bedroom, where I was lying down for a rest. I was extremely startled to see her because I didn't expect that anyone would come into the house uninvited. She said she was sorry that she had been extremely jealous of my pregnancy. Then to offer an olive branch she suddenly got on top of me—right on top of me. I think it was supposed to be a hug, but the gesture was bewildering and I felt crushed by the weight of her stocky build. I asked her to get off me, and she said good-bye and left.

Shortly after this incident my uterus began bleeding. I called the doctor, and he said to remain in bed and to come in the following day for an ultrasound. It was a tough night for me not knowing if my unborn baby was all right. The next day I found out that my tiny baby had a beating heart (thank God), but my uterus was filled with blood. There was nothing to be done at this point except to stay off my feet. The doctor ordered strict bed rest with bathroom privileges only—not an easy thing for a mother with four growing, active children in the home, but I was committed to it. The doctors arranged nursing care for me as well as help with the children and the housework. I had to learn quickly how to run the household from a horizontal position.

The children stayed near me when they weren't in school. They occupied themselves by drawing pictures for me, giving me kisses, and getting into trouble occasionally by fighting or teasing each other as children often do.

Investigated for Child Abuse

One day the doorbell rang and my home-health aide answered the door. She escorted the visitor down the hall to where I was lying on the couch with the children around me. After introducing herself the visitor said, "I am here to investigate child abuse." Just like that, without batting an eyelash.

I was stunned. As the woman continued in an accusatory tone, the children pressed closer to me. I could tell they were scared, and I knew I had to stop the woman from alarming them further. "Ma'am, please leave," I said. "You are upsetting my children. We'll call you when my husband gets home."

Thank God she left after handing me her business card. But that wasn't before she assured me that a full investigation would indeed commence.

At that time little Jessica had a bit of a shiner. One evening at dinner she had slipped off her chair and hit her head above the eyebrow against a table leg. We surmised that someone must have seen Jessica's black eye and reported us to the authorities. At first I was surprised and sad that someone would suspect us of child abuse. But thinking back, I realized that someone might have witnessed Charlie losing his temper with the children and might have thought he could have hurt Jessica.

All the teachers at the children's schools were questioned, and to my relief they all gave glowing reports. But the investigation continued. During all of the rigmarole, I suddenly remembered that the day after Jessica bumped her head on the table leg, she also tripped over a foot rest at a shoe store, where a bag of ice was obtained for Jessica's poor head. So at least there was a witness who could testify that her bruise was not the result of abuse.

It took some time for the investigation to be completed, and all the while I was on pins and needles wondering what the outcome would be. To be accused of harming my children was a tough cross for me to carry. Even after a ruling, the incident isn't closed for quite some time since it remains on one's record.

Unexpected Blessings

Meanwhile I kept to my commitment of staying on complete bed rest. The children weren't used to my not being able to do things for them, and I had a hard time getting used to it too. But the health of my unborn baby was most important.

My doctor wasn't very optimistic about my pregnancy. In fact, he said, "I wish the miscarriage would hurry up and happen." His words upset me, but remembering my previous three miscarriages it occurred to me that perhaps he was trying to protect me from further heartache. Even so, I couldn't accept that kind of logic. I was only ten weeks along when the hemorrhage occurred, and it was too early to predict an outcome. I needed to hope that the baby would be fine. I sent a letter to Mother Teresa about my situation and also asked for prayers from Father Hardon and my friends and relatives. I would be surrounded by prayer.

Being forced to stay still gave me lots of time to reflect. Though many of my thoughts were concerns about my unborn baby, I prayed to surrender to God's holy will. I had to trust God fully with my life so that He could work. He had a plan, and I needed to be open to it and ultimately to recognize that no matter what, God would bring good out of my situation.

After a while I received a wonderful letter from Mother Teresa! All her letters were wonderful, but this one was especially an answer to prayer. She wrote, "Do not be afraid. Just put yourself in the Hands of our Blessed Mother and let her take care of you. When you are afraid or sad or troubled just tell her so. She will prove herself a Mother to you." She also encouraged me to say this simple yet powerful prayer: "Mary, Mother of Jesus, make me all right; Mary, Mother of Jesus, be Mother to me now." She enclosed a Miraculous Medal and concluded, "[Mary] has done wonders for others and she will do so for you too. Just trust and pray. I am praying for you and the baby."

I had been wearing the Miraculous Medal that Mother Teresa had given me previously, but this new one was even more special because it came with her particular words and directions. I put it on and, twenty-four years later, I am still wearing it. I never take it off.

Mother Teresa's words renewed my hope. *How can she know whether the Blessed Mother will help me?* I prayed the straightforward yet poignant prayer, which in the years to come I would teach to people all around the world. Mother Teresa had taught me to lean on the Blessed Mother for everything—during that precarious pregnancy and beyond.

Motherly Inspiration

Regular home visits by the nurse and multiple ultrasounds at the doctor's office monitored the pregnancy. Each time I hoped for good news. Each time it was discovered that my baby was thriving. Thank God. But the blood in my uterus was not dissipating, which meant I remained confined to bed.

Sometimes bed rest felt like a prison of immobility. I didn't know when I would be released from my "sentence" and thought thirty-two weeks would be an impossibly long time to stay still. I needed to be patient, however, and I was thankful that my unborn baby was blossoming inside me.

One day I was inspired to envision a nine-month pregnancy as a nine-month novena. An expectant mother could dedicate the time she awaits the birth of her child to prayer and preparation. Although she might experience morning sickness, fatigue, discomfort, and other challenges, she could offer them up to God. The expectant mother could also pray specific prayers, for example, the Rosary, novenas to patron saints of pregnancy, and more.

I was so eager to describe this vision and to share it with others that I started writing about it. I didn't have a computer at the time, so my thoughts, prayers, and reflections were handwritten on pads of paper. I began to see the potential book as a prayer journal for expectant mothers. In addition to prayers and reflections for the reader, I wanted her to have space to record her own thoughts and prayers. It would become an unborn baby book!

After I finished the manuscript, I sent a copy of it to my holy friend and mentor, Mother Teresa. She thanked me for it and told me she would have her spiritual director go over it. One of her sisters in Calcutta wrote to me, "While going through the contents of your book I feel sure that many mothers will realize the great miracle of God's love and will have a greater love and respect for the unborn child."

As I continued to send my writings to Mother Teresa, my spiritual mentor encouraged me to continue writing for mothers and families. She said, "Your books on young mothers and expectant mothers are much needed. Yes, you may use some of the things I said on motherhood and family." After a while, Mother Teresa wrote the foreword to the expectant mother book! It was published years later under the title *Prayerfully Expecting: A Nine Month Novena for Mothers to Be.*

Still feeling inspired during what seemed like a very long pregnancy, I wrote additional inspirational pieces for Catholic and Christian mothers. My heart deeply desired to help mothers and families. I knew what it was like to raise Christian kids in a warped, crazy, and darkened culture and thought mothers today need all the help they can get.

I stashed all of my writings in cardboard boxes to be revisited when the time was right. For now, I needed to focus on the upcoming birth of my baby and his or her subsequent care. Sometime after the pregnancy I realized that our dear Lord slowed me down not only to preserve the health of my baby but also to give me the chance to write for mothers and expectant mothers. Years later all of the writings would be transformed into books to aid Catholic mothers on their journey to heaven. God knows what He is doing. We have to trust His wisdom and will.

Although my precarious pregnancy was difficult, God brought much good out of it. He always knows what is best for us.

During the last month of my pregnancy, I was given more freedom to get up and move around. Thank God I was no longer confined to the bed. My uterus was in better shape—just in time for childbirth.

There was another incident with Charlie. He became angry with me and lunged at me again when no one was around, and I had to run away. Again he shouted at me and chased me and wouldn't allow me to make a phone call.

Mary, Mother of Jesus, be Mother to me now.

A Gift from God

After an eventful pregnancy, Mary-Catherine Anne was finally born. I named her after the Mother of Jesus and Saint Catherine Labouré—who was visited by the Blessed Mother and given the instructions to make the Miraculous Medal—and Saint Catherine of Siena, my Dominican "friend". Her middle name was in honor of Mary's mother, Saint Anne.

Mary-Catherine was a precious and amazing gift from God. We were all thrilled. Mother Teresa said, "Thank God for His great gift of Mary-Catherine Anne." We had another little girl in the home—an incredible blessing!

When Mary-Catherine was only three and a half months old she stopped breathing. As I tried to revive her, I asked Charlie to call for the ambulance, but not believing she was in danger, he refused. I dialed a rotary wall phone while holding Mary-Catherine and still doing all I could to revive her. Jessica sensed tension and launched into a tantrum. The situation was chaotic and frightening, to say the least.

As we waited for the ambulance, Mary-Catherine began breathing, but then she stopped again. She continued this stop, start pattern, and I knew something was seriously wrong—the problem was not a matter to be resolved by administering one-time recue breathing.

Two attendants traveled in the back of the ambulance with us to the hospital. The woman took Mary-Catherine from my arms, and the man talked to me to see if I was doing all right; but I was only concerned about my baby. The female attendant said she thought the baby was merely straining to have a bowel movement. I told her I was absolutely sure that was not the reason Mary-Catherine's body was writhing as she stopped and started breathing. I told her she was my fifth baby and I was certain that something was wrong. In addition, I breastfed Mary-Catherine, which meant that unless she had a medical problem she wouldn't need to strain while having a bowel movement.

I was feeling overwhelmed all the way to the hospital because I had no doubt my baby was in distress and the person who should know better and should be helping her didn't seem to have a clue. That frightened me to the core, and I quietly prayed.

When we reached the hospital, the ambulance attendants reported to the emergency room staff that the baby was most likely only constipated. A phone call had been put through to Mary-Catherine's pediatrician, and word came back from him immediately. He said, "If Donna Cooper says her baby is not breathing, her baby is *not* breathing!"

What an ordeal! Thank God a reputable doctor came to the rescue by vouching for me as an experienced and knowledgeable mother of five. With me at her side, Mary-Catherine was hospitalized for forty-eight hours, hooked up to heart and lung monitors. She survived this episode of apnea.

For the next year Mary-Catherine's head would be elevated in her crib, on her changing table, everywhere, to prevent mucus or anything else from obstructing her breathing. I give thanks that she never had another emergency like this one.

Moving Again

Our mortgage payments had risen substantially, and Charlie wanted to move. He learned from some clients about a house that was available for a very good price. Packing up and moving a whole family while caring for a little baby was really the last thing I wanted to do, but I didn't have a choice.

We moved into a larger house in an adjoining town. It had a spacious yard for the kids to play in and was in a pleasant section of town. We did a few renovations and settled in. I was thankful that the children would be able to continue at the Catholic school they had been attending.

After a while, I began a Catholic women's group called Marian Mothers, which met each month at my house. We studied Church documents, prayed the Rosary, reached out to the needy, and strived to emulate the Blessed Mother's virtues in our lives.

Knowing of my love for horses, Charlie said he wanted to buy me one. I was completely surprised when he mentioned it. We discussed the possibility and where we might keep a horse. I liked the idea of providing the children with the wholesome activities of riding and caring for a horse, which had certainly helped with my development as I was growing up. We looked around and before long we purchased a beautiful palomino gelding named Topaz. Charlie wasn't much of a horse person, but the children and I loved him. We spent lots of time at the barn with Topaz, and the children became skilled riders in time.

Tensions with Charlie remained. His moods were both unpredictable and inescapable. I continued to pray and to seek spiritual direction from my mentors Father Hardon and Mother Teresa, as well as from my nearby friend Father Bill.

9

The Kiss of Jesus: Finding Comfort in Mother Teresa's Words

For the word of the cross is folly to those who are perishing, but to us who are being saved it is the power of God.

— First Letter of Paul to the Corinthians

Whenever I was afforded time to spend with Jesus in the Blessed Sacrament, my thoughts turned to His Passion and death on the Cross. One time in particular, when meditating on the Lord's Passion, I was deeply drawn into intense details. Although I might not have fully understood the depth of my prayer, I asked our Lord to allow me to suffer for Him and to use it for His glory.

One day my friend and spiritual director Father Bill suggested that I ask Jesus to lessen my sufferings. I suspect that, being like a father to me, he was concerned for my welfare. I told Father Bill that I couldn't ask for less suffering, that I had already made a promise to Jesus: I had told him that I would do anything He required of me.

The Great Mystery in Suffering

Suffering is shrouded in mystery. Yet the saints have often revealed the beauty and graces intertwined with suffering. In *The Imitation of Christ* Thomas à Kempis wrote: "Without doubt it is better for you ... to be tried in adversities than to have all things as you wish" and "The more spiritual progress a person makes, so much heavier will he frequently find the cross, because as his love increases, the pain of his exile also increases." He also stated, "With God, nothing that is suffered for His sake, no matter how small, can pass without reward."

Mother Teresa, in her letters published after her death, expressed the deep pain and the feeling of abandonment she experienced in a dark night of the soul. But the bottom line for her was that "in spite of all—this darkness and emptiness is not as painful as the longing for God" (*Come Be My Light*).

We were all created to long for God. We can sometimes get lost along the way in seeking Him. We become distracted, self-absorbed, confused, and sometimes we try to run and hide, afraid of the pain or the suffering we may have to endure. Thank God that He calls us back. Thank God He comes to find us.

Saint Thérèse, who was so beloved by Mother Teresa, wrote, "The cry of Jesus on the Cross sounded continually in my heart: 'I thirst!'" (*Story of a Soul*). Mother Teresa continually explained Jesus' great love through those words. Jesus, she said, incredibly thirsts for our love and wants us to thirst for His too. In searching for Him and striving to satiate His thirst for love, we might go through various periods of suffering in our lives. God calls us to learn the secret of redemptive suffering—not to waste our suffering—to unite our pain with His. As Saint John Paul II wrote, "In suffering there is concealed a particular power that draws a person interiorly close to Christ, a special grace" (*Salvifici Doloris*, 26).

Serving God in Darkness and Trial

Saint Thérèse of Lisieux also wrote, "It is good to serve God in darkness and trial! We have only this life to live by faith." Walking in faith sometimes seems like walking in the dark. I seemed to grope blindly a lot throughout my life, but with a certainty, or at least a strong hope, that there would be light—somewhere. I needed to trust God fully with my life, and I prayed to do so. When I found myself in darkness I continued to search for God there, and I strove to serve Him each day in the people He put around me, starting in my own family.

Mother Teresa's example of carrying a light of faith to others through the darkness resonated in my heart. God grants us the graces not merely to grope and to struggle through the darkness, but to be a reflection of Christ's light to others even as we endure suffering and pain in our darkness.

One day when I was at the grocery store a policeman came to my home and handcuffed my son Justin in front of his little sister Chaldea. He was then taken to the police station. I came home to a very upset Chaldea and a message that I needed to bail my son out of jail. Here was yet another trial for us to endure.

Justin was being investigated for a crime that a few of his acquaintances had committed. He had simply given them a ride from a fast food restaurant and now was linked with their wrongdoing. I paid Justin's bail, got over the shock, and dealt with the court proceedings. After what seemed like forever, Justin was cleared of all charges. I am deeply grateful for the gift of faith that sustained me during that awful ordeal, giving me the courage to offer up my troubled heart to God.

In his book *Life of Christ*, Fulton J. Sheen, the former archbishop of New York, explained the Scripture verse, "I have said this to you, that in me you may have peace. In the world you have tribulation; but be of good cheer, I have overcome the world" (Jn 16:33). Sheen wrote, "The enjoyment of peace was not inconsistent with the endurance of tribulation. Peace is in the soul, and comes from union with Him, though the body may feel pain. Trials, tribulation, anguish, anxiety are permitted by the very One Who gives peace."

Sheen revealed how his own understanding of the Cross of Christ came through personal trial. In the preface he wrote:

> *The Life of Christ* has been many years in writing. But the deeper understanding of the unity of Christ and His Cross came when Christ kept the author very close to His Cross in dark and painful hours. Learning comes from books; penetration of a mystery from suffering. It is hoped that sweet intimacy with the Crucified Christ, which trial brought, will break through these pages, giving to the reader that peace which God alone can bring to souls and enlightening them to see that every sorrow is really the "Shade of His Hand outstretched caressingly."

In the midst of persecutions and joys, Saint Peter wrote, "But rejoice in so far as you share Christ's sufferings, that you may also rejoice and be glad when his glory is revealed" (1 Pt 4:13). The Cross of Christ resides in the deepest core of a follower of Jesus. I prayed to understand more about Jesus' Passion and death and to surrender my life more deeply to Him. I had many heart-to-heart talks with our Lord, particularly when visiting Him in the Blessed Sacrament but also during the day within the heart of my home in the care of my family—between the pots and the pans, the diaper changes, and the laughter and the tears of the children.

I continued to feel drawn to meditating on the Passion of Christ. I one day felt inspired to write a reflection on The Way of the Cross and sent it to my spiritual mother, Mother Teresa. She wrote back:

Thank you for the beautiful The Way of the Cross you sent me. My gratitude is my prayer for you that you may grow in the love of God through your beautiful thoughts of prayer you write and thus share with others.

God has given you many gifts—make sure you use them for the glory of God and the good of the people. You will then make your life something beautiful for God. You have been created to be Holy.

I assure you of my prayers and I hope you pray for me also.

Keep the joy of loving Jesus ever burning in your heart and share this joy with others....

Her words deeply comforted my heart and soul.

In his book *Spiritual Life in the Modern World*, Father Hardon wrote, "Meditation on the Passion of Christ is more than reflecting on a past memory.... Is Christ in His Mystical Body suffering today? Is He being crucified today? He is." Father Hardon explained that because Christ is alive in His Body, the Church, He is suffering in those of His followers who suffer, which is all of us believers at one time or another and particularly those of us who suffer persecution for our faith in Him. "And we had better make sense of this continued crucifixion," he wrote, "if we wish to remain faithful in the following of Christ."

The continued crucifixion Father Hardon meant was the massive persecution of the Church that was taking place during the twentieth century in communist countries such as China, Vietnam, the Soviet Union, and those behind the Iron Curtain. But, he added, the Church was also being persecuted in the United States, "where so many of the laws are in open contradiction to the teachings and precepts of Christ: where the murder of unborn infants is legalized; where contraception has become a way of life; where the media continue an endless barrage of propaganda against the Catholic Church."

The saddest persecution of all, he added, is that "from within, by her own members."

The Shadow of the Cross over Me

Many of the saints have spoken about the mystery of the Cross of Christ and of redemptive suffering. When meditating on the Cross of Christ, Saint Faustina realized the need to forgive others. In her diary, *Divine Mercy in My Soul*, she wrote, "He who knows how to forgive prepares for himself many graces from God. As often as I look upon the cross, so often will I forgive with all my heart."

As tough as it is to forgive someone who hurts you, it is essential so that healing can occur and we can move forward in God's redeeming grace. God grants the graces to forgive. We need to ask Him for them—again and again. Sometimes it feels easier to resist forgiving others because it can be so difficult and painful. Forgiving someone is not accepting or condoning the harm that was done. It is forgiving the offender and becoming vulnerable before God to allow healing to occur in one's own heart. If we let go of our anger or resentment toward the person who has harmed us, we can allow the floodgates of healing to pour in. This has been a continual process in my life.

One day I noticed that a standing crucifix on a prayer table in our home had fallen over. I walked over and straightened it up and was immediately moved to get on my knees and to pray, thanking Jesus for His love and His transforming grace. I, a sinner, did not deserve it, and I felt intensely grateful for it. I knelt there for some time, praying and meditating on Jesus' great love and mercy for me. I soon shared these thoughts and more with my dear friend Mother Teresa.

Saint John Paul II explained the pivotal importance of the Cross of Christ: "If the agony of the Cross had not happened, the truth that God is Love would have been unfounded" (*Crossing the Threshold of Hope*). So often we stupidly believe that we are smarter than God. We think we know what is best for us. Saint Paul learned what really mattered through begging God to take away a source of suffering and then accepting it, trusting that God knew best: "A thorn was given me in the flesh, a messenger of Satan, to harass me, to keep me from being too elated. Three times I begged the Lord about this, that it should leave me; but he said to me, 'My grace is sufficient for you, for my power is made perfect in weakness'" (2 Cor 12:7-9). Recognizing the blessing in weakness and the power in God's mercy, he continued: "For the sake of Christ, then, I am content with weaknesses, insults, hardships, persecutions, and calamities; for when I am weak, then I am strong" (12:10).

I shared much with Father Hardon about my spiritual journey and about the difficulties in my marriage. Each time we spoke on the phone and every letter I read from him brought a deep peace to my soul. He always knew what to say to ease my heart. He consistently encouraged me and reminded me about the miraculous grace wrapped in the suffering we are called to endure in life as we strive to carry our cross. One time over the phone, in discussing spiritual matters, he said, "Our Lord is very pleased with you." His clear and simple words lifted me above the cloud of darkness I felt surrounding me. Knowing that he would never say this lightly, I wept quiet tears of joy. He also reminded me, "Stay close to our Lord. Keep at peace."

The fear of the Cross, of carrying one's cross, can be crushing. It can blind us and paralyze us or it can move us to act in an inappropriate way. For this reason we need to be careful not to allow fear to triumph over us but instead to offer our scary situations to God, asking for His help. There were many times in my life when I felt crippled by fear, yet I know without a doubt that Jesus came through for me. For instance, I recall the time I cried out to Him in utter terror when Matthew was trying to force me to shoot him in the head. God certainly worked through my weakness and vulnerability in that intense moment and revealed His awesome strength.

Pope Benedict XVI reminded us in his encyclical *Spe Salvi* that all of us at one time or another will experience suffering, that trying to avoid it is not only futile but contrary to our own happiness.

> We can try to limit suffering, to fight against it, but we cannot eliminate it. It is when we attempt to avoid suffering by withdrawing from anything that might involve hurt, when we try to spare ourselves the effort and pain of pursuing truth, love, and goodness, that we drift into a life of emptiness, in which there may be almost no pain, but the dark sensation of meaninglessness and abandonment is all the greater. It is not by sidestepping or fleeing from suffering that we are healed, but rather by our capacity for accepting it, maturing through it and finding meaning through union with Christ, who suffered with infinite love.

Perhaps when enduring pain and difficulty we can strive to remember that our Lord said, "Come to me, all who labor and are heavy laden, and I will give you rest. Take my yoke upon you, and learn from me; for I am gentle and lowly in heart, and you will find rest for your souls" (Mt 11:28–29). These words continually comforted my soul as I turned to God with my heavy burdens.

Throughout the years I knew Mother Teresa, I continued to share my heart fully with her. She always responded with profound words intertwined with great love and generous prayers for me and my family. I felt blessed knowing a living saint whose sandals were firmly on the ground. As I have mentioned before, Mother Teresa's head wasn't in some lofty cloud somewhere. She was well aware of the realities of life; she knew all about pain and suffering. Even more important was her deep understanding about the value of suffering when united to our Lord's. Mother Teresa's words were a great comfort. In a letter to me she wrote, "Jesus shares His love with you and shares His suffering and pain." She continued with amazing clarity and wisdom, teaching me a deeply valuable lesson:

> He is a God of love and does not want His children to suffer, but when you accept your pain, suffering, death and resurrection your pain becomes redemptive for yourself and for others.... Be assured of my prayers. Christ calls us to be one with Him in love through unconditional surrender to His plan for us. Let us allow Jesus to use us without consulting us by taking what He gives and giving what He takes.

I recalled Mother Teresa's words often and strove to accept God's holy will in my life. Her letter let me in on an amazing mystery and reality of Christian love: "Suffering is the sharing in the Passion of Christ. Suffering is the kiss of Jesus, a sign that you have come so close to Jesus on the Cross that He can kiss you. Do offer some of your sufferings for us and our people."

The many trials of my childhood and my adult life—dramatic or mundane, brief or drawn out, secret or exposed for all to see—had wrapped within them all along a deeper meaning and a supernatural purpose. Jesus has kissed me. Wow.

10

Divorce: Agony and Liberation

So we do not lose heart. Though our outer man is wasting away, our inner man is being renewed every day. For this slight momentary affliction is preparing for us an eternal weight of glory beyond all comparison, because we look not to the things that are seen but to the things that are unseen; for the things that are seen are transient, but the things that are unseen are eternal.

—Second Letter of Paul to the Corinthians

Charlie agreed to try counseling again. When asked if he would ever harm his wife, Charlie vehemently answered, "No! Of course not! I love Donna. I would never ever hurt her!" I couldn't bear it. Maybe he did love me and did not intend to hurt me, but when he lost his temper he did do harm. If he could not admit this, I knew that my situation wasn't going to change.

One Sunday morning while getting ready for Mass, Charlie started yelling at me. He stormed out the door, ushering the kids to the car. I followed them outside and was just seated in the front passenger seat when Charlie sped up the driveway, before I had even closed the door or buckled my seatbelt. The children were frightened and started to cry. They pleaded for him to slow down, but with steely eyes and hands tightly gripping the steering wheel he raced down the winding roads to the church. If I hadn't been so afraid for the kids and me, I might have chuckled at the absurdity of the situation—Charlie going crazy while en route to Mass. I turned around in my seat, directly facing the children, and as calmly as I could told them not to worry, that I was going to talk to the priest when we got to church. They needed to know that I was going to make sure that they would be protected from harm. Before that moment, I don't think they felt confident that they would be.

As soon as we arrived, I went straight to the sacristy and told our priest what was happening—that the kids and I were feeling terrorized by Charlie's rages. I then returned to our pew. I knew right then and there that I would not allow Charlie to terrorize us again. We had endured many similar incidents prior to this one, but I resolved that we shouldn't have to endure them any longer. Charlie had to get help. He never received any type of exit counseling after coming out of the cult.

I tried to hang on to some powerful words from Scripture:

> Therefore, since we are justified by faith, we have peace with God through our Lord Jesus Christ. Through him we have obtained access to this grace in which we stand, and we rejoice in our hope of sharing the glory of God. More than that, we rejoice in our sufferings, knowing that suffering produces endurance, and endurance produces character, and character produces hope, and hope does not disappoint us, because God's love has been poured into our hearts through the Holy Spirit who has been given to us. (Rom 5:1–5)

God would bring good out of the suffering—somehow. I had to believe that.

My Nightmare Begins

I discussed with our priest the frightening experience in the car, and then with a legal expert, and I was advised to seek a restraining order. Some people warned me that even though a restraining order is supposed to protect, in reality it is only a piece of paper and that not much can actually prevent one person from harming another. I had to go to the courthouse to apply for the restraining order, and that alone caused me to tremble. *Will I see him there?* It was where he practiced law. Charlie might go ballistic if he thought his secret would be out.

Typically when a restraining order is approved by the court, a sheriff serves the person with an order to appear in court two weeks later. In the meantime, he is ordered to stay clear of the party who has filed for protection. In my case, what happened was the beginning of my nightmare with the court system, otherwise known in some circles as the "good ol' boys' club".

I would find out later that a court clerk tipped off Charlie and told him I had been to the courthouse and had filed the complaint against him—the court that was supposed to protect the one seeking the protection did the complete opposite. The judge ordered Charlie and me to appear *that very afternoon*! Of course Charlie would have legal representation. He had his law partner, and he was also thoroughly knowledgeable in the law since he was an attorney. I had no one. It was such an unfair situation. Yet, I had to hope and pray for the best.

I made arrangements for the kids to be cared for by a friend and I showed up at court at the appropriate time. The hearing was intense, and sure enough Charlie's partner accompanied him for support and legal representation. The old judge (who was nicknamed "the odd duck" for his sometimes peculiar rulings) wrote out a "joint" restraining order: for the next few weeks Charlie would have to leave the premises but could come to the house every evening for dinner, and I was to do his laundry too. *What kind of protection is this?* My plan to get help from the court system totally backfired. Still, I had to move forward with hope and prayer. There would be another court-ordered hearing in a few weeks.

Separation

We met again in court for a hearing, and the judge discontinued the restraining order. *Where does this leave me?* I pondered. Charlie was currently living out of the house, and no longer paying the bills, but he came over whenever he wanted to.

In an attempt to save some money, I arranged for someone to colease our horse, which granted riding privileges in exchange for a fee. This would reduce our time with our dearly loved horse, but the arrangement paid for most of the cost of boarding Topaz at his stable, which was a big relief.

I went in for a medical check-up and ended up telling my obstetrician that I was seeking a legal separation from my husband. I also expressed my fear at how Charlie might react. My doctor knew him and strongly cautioned me. He advised me to get an alarm system installed in my house, because he feared that Charlie might attack me. I questioned whether an alarm system was really necessary, but my doctor was a wise man.

What he told me next caused me to tremble all over. He said one of his patients sought a separation from her husband and was murdered and put through a wood chipper (a famous case in Connecticut)! The conversation frightened me to the core as I considered the possible consequences of separating from Charlie, but I still felt separation was absolutely necessary. Charlie was harming us, and I no longer trusted him.

I did some research and sought counsel. Then, with equal parts trepidation and determination, I filed for a legal separation. I knew that the Church teaches that at times a separation is best for all parties. Specifically, the *Catechism of the Catholic Church* states, "The *separation* of spouses while maintaining the marriage bond can be legitimate in certain cases provided for by canon law" (2383). Additionally, it says, "If civil divorce remains the only possible way of ensuring certain legal rights, the care of the children, or the protection of inheritance, it can be tolerated and does not constitute a moral offence" (2383).

I didn't go so far as to ask for a divorce. I still hoped that with counseling there might be a chance to save the marriage. But Charlie immediately countersued for divorce. Thus, an intense, protracted legal battle began. The divorce proceedings took over three years because Charlie, who could use his power in the court system at no cost to himself, insisted upon custody of the children, which I opposed. He filed motion after motion against me, criticizing me and accusing me of all kinds of things, in his attempts to win the case. Each time, I needed to defend myself, and at times without an attorney to represent me. The case dragged on for about ten years more due to Charlie's appeal of the final outcome and the motions he continued to file against me.

I soon found out that the court system does not protect the innocent children or the victimized spouse. In my humble opinion, it serves the one with the most money and power. Perhaps it seems that I am exaggerating, but there are countless cases in which this seems to be true.

Many reputable people recommended that I go underground. Perhaps if I had had only one small baby who could have been uprooted easily, I might have considered their advice. But I had five growing children. With that many it would have been much too difficult to run and hide. I would have been constantly looking over my shoulder until the kids were all of legal age, because Charlie had the power and the money to search for me and to take the children away from me. I was not willing to risk that, as painful as it was to endure the proceedings and the uncertainty of the outcome.

Agonizing Court Proceedings

There should have been no reason for me to fear that the kids or I could be hurt in the court proceedings. After all, I was a devoted stay-at-home mother, involved in the care of all five of my children. I was deeply devoted to family life, was a churchgoer, and raised the children as upright citizens. Yet suddenly, I was being accused of hurting the ones I loved. Allegedly, I was programming or brainwashing the children against Charlie. Yet I had never once bad-mouthed him to the kids.

Charlie hired a hotshot attorney, in addition to his partner, to represent him. The new guy was an expert in divorce law and had gotten his own wife put away in a mental institution and had won the custody of their children. That was the kind of expertise I was up against. Charlie was determined to prove that I was mentally ill so that he could take the children away. The whole ordeal was the worst nightmare of my life.

Meanwhile, the children and I received a terrible blow. We managed to get away from the stress of the divorce at a small county fair in the town where we used to live. The six of us enjoyed the sights and the sounds of farm animals, country wares, and fair exhibitions. But when we arrived home I received a shocking telephone call, informing me that our horse Topaz was dead. He had been shot in the stomach and left in a field to bleed to death.

Who would do such a thing? I asked myself. *What will I tell the kids?* Chaldea had become particularly close to Topaz. Our horse had been a needed distraction for her because Charlie picked on her the most. I wondered why until he said she was a carbon copy of me.

After I hung up the phone, I told the children that Topaz had been shot. I tried to lessen the shock and pain by suggesting that a hunter might have mistaken him for a deer. I didn't want them to suffer more than was necessary by thinking that someone had deliberately killed him.

Word got around town fast. The newspaper called to ask for my opinion. They also asked for a photo of Topaz. It was a big deal in a small town that a family horse was mysteriously shot and killed. After the story hit the front page of the newspaper, I was plagued with inquiries.

"Did your husband shoot your horse?" one store owner asked me when I was shopping.

My jaw dropped before I answered, "No, I don't think he would ever do that."

Then the children's attorney called me to ask what had happened. She had already heard about it from Charlie. She said she had no doubt that Charlie did it, or paid someone to do it, because he was always complaining to her that I was spending too much money to feed the horse. I told her that we couldn't and shouldn't speculate, and for the record I was coleasing the horse and didn't have to pay for board.

Shortly after, Charlie filed a motion that accused me of terrorizing the kids by telling them that he had killed the family horse and the family cat. *How did he know about our cat?* I wondered. Our cat had suddenly disappeared just before our horse was shot. Chaldea had been particularly fond of the cat too.

I had to defend myself constantly against Charlie's false accusations. At times I had an attorney to represent me, and at other times I represented myself. When giving my own defense, I would be up against several attorneys at once. The experience was intimidating, to say the least.

In those moments, I often thought about this Scripture verse: "And when they bring you to trial and deliver you up, do not be anxious beforehand about what you are to say; but say whatever is given you in that hour, for it is not you who speak, but the Holy Spirit" (Mk 13:11).

I prayed constantly to the Holy Spirit for guidance. I needed to trust God with my life; I needed to continue to surrender to Him. He would provide the perfect outcome. It wasn't easy hanging on to that conviction when it seemed as if hell was breaking loose around me. But, I absolutely knew it was the only way.

When it was hard to formulate the words to pray, I simply offered my heart to God. When possible, I would slip away to the Blessed Sacrament at church. When I was confined to the household, which was the majority of the time, I would pray quietly and do my best to trust God. A very large painting of Saint Rita, the saint of the impossible as she is sometimes called, hung in my laundry room. I bought it at a thrift shop of all places! At times I found refuge by peering at the painting as I did the family's laundry. I felt I could relate to Rita in some way—perhaps because she suffered greatly in her marriage and because she interceded for hopeless situations.

Under the Microscope

As part of the divorce proceedings, Charlie and I had to undergo psychological examinations. I didn't mind the tests because I felt I had nothing to hide. I expected the results to show that I am a stable person and they did. But I was surprised to find out later that one report mildly criticized me: for apologizing for being a few minutes late for our session, by saying that I had to change a diaper just as we were leaving for the hour-long trip to the office. It was said I might have been blaming someone else (the baby) for my tardiness. I never knew how anything I said would be interpreted, even an apology for being a few minutes late.

Everyone in the family received court-ordered counseling. The first of the children's counselors, however, never got a chance to express her opinions to the judge. When she arrived for a hearing, I overheard Charlie's attorney say, "Don't let her get her ass on the stand!" He didn't let her; Charlie's attorney succeeded in establishing that she was not an expert witness in that particular courthouse.

I went into each counseling session hoping that an expert would see what was going on in the kids' lives and provide them with the help they needed. The first counselor seemed ready and able to do this, but the one who replaced her began our first session with, "Okay, who is a half and who is a step?"

What? I couldn't believe it. We had never referred to halves or steps or anything of the sort. As far as I was concerned, all of my children came from the same womb—mine—and they were all brothers and sisters to each other. I didn't want anyone to plant doubts in their minds about that. Given that our family had particular challenges it was understandable that the counselor would seek to know which children were from a previous marriage. But to ask such a question in front of the children, in such a way, did not inspire confidence in me.

I had hoped that the court would see Charlie's true colors after viewing the results of his psychological tests. But Charlie was able to use the court system to his advantage. He sought the judges and the experts he knew were most likely to rule in his favor. Yes, his psychological testing revealed some problems, but that didn't mean they would be taken into account. That would depend on whether my lawyer was able to bring them to light.

At some point I sought out counseling for myself at a Catholic Charities center that offered appointments on a sliding scale. My counselor said she couldn't understand why I didn't show anger toward Charlie and encouraged me to possess a hatred for him, assuring me that it would be good for me. *What? Why should I allow the devil to hoodwink me with vindictiveness and even hatred?* Saint Maximilian Kolbe observed that the worst crimes that were committed in the Nazi prison camps were when the victimized prisoners felt that they should get even. *No, this is not God's way.* I was not going to feed the fire by desiring to be angry in the way the counselor suggested. I did not want my heart hardened. I stopped going to that counselor after a few sessions, and I knew I would have to pray hard to be able to forgive Charlie for what he was doing.

A strange language seemed to be spoken in court. I could never really honestly say what was on my mind. When I would try to speak the truth, I would be cut off mid-sentence, due to objections by the opposing attorney that my statements were only hearsay or unacceptable for some other reason.

Everything I said or did was measured, calculated and often twisted into something dramatically different from what I intended. Charlie knew exactly how to paint a picture of me to suit his needs. I wondered whether the judge believed him, especially after I heard that a judge usually believes about 50 percent of what each side says.

One day Charlie saw me at a bus stop and tried to grab Joseph out of my arms. Joseph was scared and asked him to stop, but Charlie twisted my arm and Joseph's arm and took the boy for a moment. He handed Joseph back to me, got in his fancy car and left. A parent standing nearby witnessed the incident. That evening the pediatrician examined Joseph's arm. When she asked what had happened, little Joseph said sadly, "My daddy twisted my arm."

I filed for a warrant for Charlie's arrest in hopes that it would help to end the madness. But the warrant was declined. And because I didn't have the funds to fight this in court, my attorney chose not to subpoena the pediatrician.

My one and only witness of the abuse backed out too. Charlie had approached her at the bus stop shortly afterward and said, "You didn't see anything, right?" Over the next few days she was followed by a detective and received phone calls from Charlie's law partner. The intimidation tactics worked; the woman became frightened. She had been subpoenaed by my attorney to testify in court. But, she called me one day, crying and saying that she was concerned about the safety of her children and herself. I couldn't ask her to continue as my witness and dropped the matter. My heart sank. *Mary, Mother of Jesus, be Mother to me now.*

At a hearing shortly after the incident, one of Charlie's attorneys asked me, "Isn't it true that it was you who twisted Joseph's arm?"

I was mortified. I could not believe that he had reversed the truth and was accusing me of hurting Joseph.

"No, it is not true," I answered.

So many motions were filed against me and delivered by the sheriff along with subpoenas ordering me to court that I didn't want to answer the front door anymore. The long ordeal was so exhausting and mind-boggling that I was losing weight and feeling fatigued. Keeping up with my duties as a mother and the court proceedings took everything I had. With nothing left over for Saint Joseph's Corner, I had to close my beloved shop. Could I possibly remember or even take time to think about the weight of this affliction compared to the "eternal weight of glory"? I had to.

Visitation

The first time Charlie came to pick up the kids for a visitation, there was a big hullabaloo. Charlie pulled into the driveway, and two more cars followed behind him. Charlie's parents were in one car and his sister in another. The children felt surrounded! Chaldea was very concerned about Charlie taking the baby, Mary-Catherine, when he had never even fed her before and didn't know much about her care. Feeling conflicted and fearful, she called 911 without my knowing. This action she had learned from a counselor. The police arrived, and to our relief Charlie was asked to leave along with his family members. I was subpoenaed the following day for a hearing. Charlie was trying to hold me in contempt of court because of what had occurred. Likening the drama to a famous battle, the judge threw out the motion. He said he didn't blame the kids for being scared.

The fact is, the children did not want to see their father. They were upset and frightened by his behavior. The older ones, who weren't his biological children, refused to visit him. Eventually they were let off the hook by the court because they were old enough to decide the matter for themselves. But that was after many appointments, children's attorneys, and hearings. The younger ones were forced to go, however. If they didn't see him, I could be held in contempt of court. I tried to facilitate the process, but it was sometimes nearly impossible. Watching the children cry hysterically or suffer from panic broke my heart.

Eventually, the court ordered me to take the kids to Charlie's town-house, since it was believed that the exchange away from their home might be easier on them. But several times Charlie asked the police to be present because, according to him, I was refusing to cooperate. The presence of the police made the visits even harder on the children. Jessica would get a stomach ache, and Joseph would become visibly anxious. One time a police officer asked Joseph directly if he wanted to stay with his father. Joseph politely answered, "No, thank you", and he was allowed to come back home with me that day.

One time Charlie was angrily threatening me over the phone about the visitation that would occur later that day. Afterward I shared my concerns about our safety with a friend who happened to call. She suggested that I call the police. I explained to her that the reason I didn't want to bring the police into it was because Charlie had done that so often and that it had made the kids even more afraid. She said she really believed that I should. I prayed about it and decided to call the police for advice. I asked if they could be on alert in case I needed them. The officer told me that they would have to be at the scene. I agreed to it but specifically asked that they try to be discreet so as not to frighten the children.

Later that afternoon, I drove the kids to the church parking lot (which had become a neutral place to do the exchanges). Charlie got out of his car and began to yell at me. There was no one around to witness it—or so I thought. Charlie seemed to become more and more agitated as he moved toward me, his arms flailing around as he threatened me. Out of the corner of my eye, I detected a patrol car that had pulled into the parking lot from the other direction and was keeping a distance. Before long the car drove closer, and I became suddenly afraid that Charlie would be even angrier because he would figure out that I had called the police.

Charlie took off with the younger children, and the police officer offered me his business card. I wasn't sure why, but I soon found out. There was another hearing coming up. Now that I had the officer's name on his business card, my attorney could call him. The officer who had been at the scene was subpoenaed. It turned out that he had video-taped the entire encounter. I was thoroughly heartened knowing that there would now be evidence showing Charlie in action and how it affected the children.

At the next hearing, as I eagerly waited for it to begin, I hoped and prayed for justice to prevail—finally. But instead the judge opted not to watch the video. I was flabbergasted! He did listen to testimony from the police officer, and though the officer was cut off numerous times by Charlie's attorney, his points about Charlie's inappropriate behavior became part of the court record.

Flash from the Past

At one hearing I was shocked to see my ex-husband Chris on the wit-ness stand. Charlie's attorney questioned him, but finally, thank God, the judge said he was throwing out all of Chris' testimony and wouldn't allow it to continue in his courtroom. He said he wasn't going to allow anyone to dig up an old case. (Chris' parental rights had been terminated by Charlie himself.)

The next shock came when I stepped outside the courtroom during a break. Many of Chris' family members, whom I hadn't seen in years, had been invited by Charlie to the courthouse and were gathered in the hallway. I had no inkling at the time that in years to come, by God's grace, I would minister to three of Chris' relatives. More on that later.

Losing Our House and Almost My Children

Throughout the lengthy court proceedings many a lawyer quit on me. They told me that they couldn't keep up with Charlie's continual litigation, which ate up any retainer I had given them. Financially I was at a huge disadvantage. Yet I needed to trust God completely.

Our house went into foreclosure because I didn't have any money for the mortgage payments. Charlie had been court-ordered to pay it, but somehow got away with not paying. To add insult to injury, the mortgage holder's law office sent a couple of people over to our home unannounced. I peered out the front window to see them pounding a huge foreclosure sign into the ground in our front yard. It was quite an embarrassment. Meanwhile, Charlie was completely up-to-date on all the payments on his townhouse.

At first, I borrowed money from friends and family members to try to keep the roof over our heads and to stop the foreclosure process. But even with their help it soon became impossible to make the payments. Charlie filed a motion with the court asking for full custody of the children since their home was in foreclosure. He said I couldn't provide for them.

I tried my best to convince the court to hold Charlie financially responsible for keeping the children in their home; but Charlie testified that the house should be sold so that there would be money for their care, and the judge ordered it to be sold.

I felt overwhelmed. My life seemed to be falling apart, but I was not going to give up the hope that there was a solution somewhere—somehow. I prayed and hung on to my faith in God. He would see us through.

Though I knew in my heart that God had a plan, it pretty much killed me each time a realtor showed up at my door with potential buyers. A bustling household full of children was now expected to be in pristine condition at all times to accommodate the realtors and their clients. If not, I would be reported as uncooperative.

Once again I had to pack everything and find a new home. I knew that the Lord who took care of the birds (Mt 6:26) would take care of us too. If He allowed us to suffer a bit, He would provide the graces. I had to believe that God would provide.

A rental house became available in our little town, and I was able to secure it and move us in. Unfortunately, one of the movers robbed my purse of the cash I had set aside to pay for meals for a couple of days while we settled in. I found my wallet the day after the move in a pile of stuff that was left behind at our old address. Upon questioning by the police, the moving man admitted to stealing the money. He paid me back in dribs and drabs, but never finished paying the debt.

As we settled into our new home, one of the first things I hung on the wall was the old black-and-white picture of the Sacred Heart of Jesus that hung in every place we lived. I had bought it at a thrift store for only two dollars and have treasured it ever since.

I was looking forward to some peace now that we were out of the old house filled with memories. But before long, unexpectedly, Charlie was out in the driveway leaning on his car horn. He was supposed to meet us for visitation in the church parking lot, but instead he had come to the house. He had gone to the courthouse and filed a motion stating that I was refusing him visitation and that therefore he needed to go to the house for the kids. Because the older children who chose not to see him felt harassed, the court ordered him to stay away from the house.

Charlie testified that he wanted sole custody of all five of my children because the children should not be with me. He would allow me some visitation rights, he said, and he would hire a nanny. He told the court that the children would be very comfortable with the woman he would hire because she had previously stayed at our house. This woman was one of the former cult members who had stayed with us.

Oh my! Is this the kiss of Jesus too? I had to listen quietly to this proposal without so much as raising an eyebrow or rolling my eyes, for which I could get thrown out of the courtroom depending on which judge was on the bench.

What was even more ridiculous to my mind was Charlie's attempt to take a nursing child away from her mother. But crazy outcomes sometimes result from court proceedings. One never knew what the judge would rule. All I could do was pray and defend my children and myself as best I could.

During this time I was consoled by a letter from Mother Teresa.

> I am sorry to hear of the suffering you have to undergo. Jesus loves you and though He is the Lord of all—He cannot interfere with the gift of free will He has given to man. Jesus shares His love with you and shares His suffering and pain. He is a God of love and does not want His children to suffer, but when you accept your pain, suffering, death and resurrection your pain becomes redemptive for yourself and for others.... Be assured of my prayers. Christ calls us to be one with Him in love through unconditional surrender to His plan for us. Let us allow Jesus to use us without consulting us by taking what He gives and giving what He takes. God love you and bless you.

I was able to speak with my beautiful spiritual mother on the phone as well. I called the motherhouse in Calcutta, India, hoping to reach her and she picked up the phone! She could have been any place in the world. I was blessed with an unforgettable conversation with Mother Teresa in which she promised her prayers for the upcoming legal proceedings. Her words sustained me in the darkness that surrounded me.

God was giving me courage. Just before our case moved forward to a full trial (yes, a full trial!), I had to do something to protect the kids and me. It had become clear that my current attorney was not capable of representing me properly. He had also inappropriately yelled at me on a few occasions. It was very tough for me to do, but I had to dismiss him from the case and told the court that I needed a couple of weeks' time to find a new attorney. That would be a miracle in itself. The court allowed me to proceed in this way. I found a new attorney who seemed promising, but we had such a short time to prepare before the trial would begin.

The first day of the trial arrived. My attorney warned me that Charlie had many witnesses lined up to testify against me and that he was hellbent on proving that I was unstable. On the way into the courtroom she whispered that I had better settle for joint custody. If I didn't, she said, the court-appointed psychologist, who was supposedly friendly with the judge, might say something incriminating against me. I couldn't imagine what it could be, but I had seen Charlie's team in action before. I reminded myself of some powerful words in Scripture.

> Finally, be strong in the Lord and in the strength of his might. Put on the whole armor of God, that you may be able to stand against the wiles of the devil. For we are not contending against flesh and blood, but against the principalities, against the powers, against the world rulers of this present darkness, against the spiritual hosts of wickedness in the heavenly places. (Eph 6:10–12)

By God's grace, I stood my ground and would not agree to joint custody. I saw that I was engaged in a spiritual battle, and I continued to ask God for strength and courage. I needed them.

As the hearing began, beads of perspiration were rolling down my skin beneath my dress. My heart pounded. I was in agony as testimony stretched on for hours. I was called to the witness stand to testify and to be cross-examined by Charlie's attorney. I sat there next to the judge's bench trying to be as calm as possible. I sat up straight. I could feel my right hand tremble as I held it up and gave my oath to tell the truth. I hoped that no one noticed I was shaking. This was certainly not the first time I would testify on the witness stand. I had been doing it for a few years now. But I felt I was up against evil, and this was the final trial to determine what would happen to the kids.

It was excruciating and intense. At times during my testimony I held back tears and at other times a few slipped out. But I knew without a doubt that God was with me. He wasn't going to let me down no matter how scary things looked.

When the court-appointed psychologist got on the witness stand and testified, I was appalled and frightened all at once as I heard my words and those of the children twisted against me. I could feel my heart beating in my chest. *Will the judge believe him? After all, my attorney said they were friends. Will my attorney be able to set the record straight?* These questions raced through my mind, and I continued to pray silently.

It was time for the second children's attorney to cross-examine the psychologist. The court had appointed an additional attorney for the kids since the case was very complicated. As she began to question the psychologist, I didn't know what to expect; this attorney was difficult to read. She eventually caught the psychologist in an inconsistency and was able to demonstrate it to the court. Seeing her skillfully bring the truth to light gave me the chills. I was ecstatically happy at what had transpired.

The judge reprimanded the psychologist several times for saying "I guess" instead of "It is my professional opinion" about a certain matter. He was being discredited as a witness. Prayers were being answered big time! But the ordeal wasn't over yet; we had several more days of trial to get through. In the end, however, the court awarded me sole legal and physical custody of the children. Charlie appealed the decision, but he lost in the higher court too. He got the house out from under us and all of the other assets and money, but I was granted what mattered the most—the children.

Not long afterward Charlie remarried, and the battle for the children would continue for many years. Charlie filed numerous motions against me and hired detectives to follow me around. For now, however, I rejoiced in the victory and the justice God had won for us. I needed to keep putting one foot in front of the other to walk in faith, trusting in Him to provide for all of our needs, both spiritually and physically.

In a letter to one of her sisters, Saint Thérèse of Lisieux once remarked, "I find that trials help very much in detaching us from this earth. They make us look higher than this world. Here below, nothing can satisfy us. We cannot enjoy a little rest except in being ready to do God's will."

III

Discovery: God Is Always Present

11

Jesus in the Distressing Disguise of the Poorest of the Poor

If sometimes our poor people have had to die of starvation, it is not because God didn't care for them, but because you and I didn't give, were not instruments of love in the hands of God, to give them that bread, to give them that clothing; because we did not recognize Him, when once more Christ came in distressing disguise—in the hungry man, in the lonely man, in the homeless child, seeking for shelter.

—*Mother Teresa*

Jesus hadn't stopped *kissing* me.

We got hit with a very bad stomach virus, and Mary-Catherine became dehydrated and needed to be hospitalized for the first time since she was a baby. Aware that Mary-Catherine was frightened, the pediatrician was very caring and undertook the task of starting the intravenous fluids herself. Something that should have taken a few minutes took over an hour because Mary-Catherine's tiny veins kept collapsing. Because I was a single mother, the doctor persuaded the hospital staff to let Joseph (who also was sick and needed my care) to stay with me in Mary-Catherine's hospital room. In a couple of days Mary-Catherine was better, and so was Joseph.

When it was time to renew my rental lease, my landlord informed me that he was going to be selling the house to his relative. We had to move within thirty days. It would be a mammoth job to pack up the entire family—again—along with the preschool program that I had begun running from my home. I began scouring the ads in the paper and praying a novena to dear Saint Joseph to ask his intercession and help in finding a suitable home. Meanwhile, another calamity arrived.

139

One day I received a phone call informing me that Joseph's eye had been seriously injured at a friend's house. A playmate had whacked a badminton birdie into Joseph's eye at close range, and the parents were bringing Joseph home. I was on pins and needles as I waited. When they arrived, Joseph was in excruciating pain. He also had one green eye and one dark brown eye! Normally, both were green. The blood that had pooled in his injured eye had turned it almost black. I was beside myself. Poor Joseph! We immediately took him to the hospital. The doctor informed us that the injury was extremely serious and that Joseph might need surgery. We had to wait for the eye specialist to make a more thorough examination. The waiting seemed endless. I prayed my Rosary on my fingertips and stayed by Joseph's side, comforting him.

The specialist finally arrived and thoroughly examined Joseph's eye. An anesthesiologist friend from church entered the room to see if he was needed before he left for the night. The attending doctor told him that he could leave, that Joseph wouldn't need surgery. I exhaled and shed a few quiet tears. Seeing someone I knew, especially a Christian, was comforting. He gave me a hug and then was on his way.

Joseph wasn't allowed to lie flat due to the blood in his eye and the danger of certain pressures affecting his brain. Instead he had to sit in a reclined chair for two weeks and have several medications put into his eye throughout the day. He was a very obedient patient. I was so relieved and happy when he was back to normal.

It was difficult handling these crises on my own as a single mother, but I truly believed that God gave me strength in every instance. Saint Teresa of Avila once said, "Observe that we gain more in a single day by trials which come to us by God and our neighbor than we would in ten years by penances and other exercises which we take up of ourselves." We must trust that God as the Divine Physician knows exactly what we need and when we need it. Although hard at times to accept, openness to and acceptance of His will for us is essential for our growth in holiness. "Holiness is not the luxury of a few," Mother Teresa would say, "but a simple duty for you and me."

Moving On with My Life

I continued to raise my children as a single mother for many more years. Despite the rigid visitation schedule, the continued court proceedings, and the other challenges, it was a time of sharing countless joys with my children—helping with the finishing touches on hair and make-up, tying neckties, and pinning on corsages or boutonnieres before school proms and other occasions; cheering on the children at their school and sports events; being misty-eyed over their academic accomplishments and at their graduations. Life was full!

Raising my children and conducting my preschool classes kept me quite busy. I was also involved in my parish as a religious educator and did some Catholic writing whenever I had the chance.

I soon faced another hurdle. My new landlord tried to sue me for nonpayment of rent. He had doubled my rental fee without warning. We didn't have a written lease. When I questioned the change, he had me subpoenaed. Thankfully, the court found me innocent of the accusations, but I still had to move out.

A New Chapter Unfolds

After Charlie married again, he filed a petition with the Church for an annulment, and the decree of nullity was granted. I was happy to partake in the process again so that I could be open to the healing I knew it would bring.

Years later, when I least expected it, I met a man named Dave. We hit it off on our first Sunday afternoon "blind" date, which took place after weeks of emails and phone calls. We continued dating, and went on to enjoy a happy courtship for a few years. During this special time I was overjoyed to introduce Dave to Father Bill, who gave the relationship his "stamp of approval". Our marriage in the Church took place about ten years after I had separated from Charlie. Dear Father Bill concelebrated our nuptial Mass with the pastor at Saint Mary's, the parish where I grew up and received First Penance, First Holy Communion and Confirmation. My five children were all part of our special day as the maid of honor, bride's maids, ushers, and a reader. Justin "gave me away". I was joyfully moving on with my life.

One Sunday afternoon Dave and I noticed an intriguing ad for a house in the nearby countryside. We inquired and before long, Dave, the children, and I settled into that house. I'll never forget the first time we drove along the windy dirt roads to see it. At one point, a great blue heron that was perched at the side of the road took off and majestically flew right over our car. That breathtaking sight clinched the deal for me. I looked forward to living in such a beautiful environment.

Dave moved his business to the area. After unpacking and hanging up the old black-and-white picture of the Sacred Heart of Jesus in our new living room, I called Father Bill and asked him to bless our new home. In our new bedroom I placed the large two-foot statue of Saint Joseph that had previously stood watch in Saint Joseph's Corner. It was a reminder of my beloved apostolate, but more importantly, it was a reminder of Saint Joseph's intercession in my life. He had come to my aid many a time in my domestic church.

After that, I set out to dig a vegetable garden in the backyard. Before long, I was growing all kinds of organic vegetables including hundreds of garlic plants, which I believe to be healthful and medicinal. We all thoroughly enjoyed the peace and quiet in our rural area, as well as the wildlife we observed each day.

I can't tell you that my life suddenly became a happily-ever-after story in that there were no more challenges to endure. Life is by and large a crooked path with many unexpected twists and turns along the way. But God has a unique plan for each of us. We need to surrender to it. God had been showing me all along that His grace is always enough to get me through anything. The essential questions we need to ask ourselves when faced with challenges are these: What will we do? How will we respond to it all? Will we be open to God's grace and respond to others with Christ's love?

My life is much better than any fairy tale. Because of God's mysterious ways, I possess a deep joy in my heart and soul, and I want to continue to embrace the unique plan that God has for me.

Books and More Books

I had been writing Catholic articles whenever I could fit them into my schedule. After careful reflection and prayer, I decided to retire from my preschool program and to devote myself to full-time writing. Mother Teresa and Father Hardon had encouraged me to continue writing. Mother Teresa had said that she prayed my writing would "do much good" and that I should do it "for the glory of God and the good of the people". Father Hardon had given me positive feedback and had reminded me that "many mothers are overwhelmed" and need encouragement and inspiration.

After many years of storing away my writings in cardboard boxes, I heard from a publisher who asked if I would be interested in writing a prayer book for Catholic mothers. They had seen some of my writing in the past, and I was thrilled to be invited to write for them. Before long, I signed my first book contract and got to work. Dave was very supportive of my writing work, and I thoroughly enjoyed the writing process, praying as I wrote that God would use my words for His glory and to help and encourage mothers of all ages. I drew from some ideas I had during my long bed rest while pregnant with Mary-Catherine.

I'll never forget the day that the copies of my first book arrived. Dave came in from the mailbox, and suspecting that the contents of the small package might be my first book, he placed the parcel on a pillow and ceremoniously carried it to me in the kitchen. I smiled at his presentation and eagerly opened the package to find two copies of *Catholic Prayer Book for Mothers*! I handed a copy to Dave to peruse while I checked out the other. As Dave read through the dedication, he wept upon seeing the words addressed to him: "Dedicated with great love.... To my husband, David, for his love and support. He is the wind beneath my wings."

Less than a week after my first book was released, it made the top ten Catholic bestseller list announced by *Publishers Weekly*. I was utterly astonished. My thoughts returned immediately to my sitting in front of my computer, typing the words of the prayer book, and having absolutely no idea about its future impact. I had thought at the time that I would be happy enough if I could reach one reader's heart. I simply prayed as I wrote. God's ways are amazing.

God was putting a passionate desire in my heart to share Him with others in my writings and talks. It wouldn't be until many years later that I would begin to share bits and pieces of my personal life when writing about the faith. Not until this book, *The Kiss of Jesus*, would I reveal so many of my experiences and the secrets I had never shared before.

A ministry began to unfold—one I had never dreamed, much less planned. The speaking part of it started when Father Paul Murphy, pastor of Saint Mary's in Ridgefield, Connecticut, asked me if I would speak to a group of women at his parish. As I accepted, I was struck with the sense that God was going to keep me busy with speaking engagements.

This was something I hadn't thought about prior to Father Murphy's invitation. After all I was very quiet and shy as a young girl. But God was asking me to venture out of my comfort zone. He wanted me to move through any fear of public speaking to reach others. I didn't quite know how I would accomplish this task, but I didn't worry. I believed it would all unfold the way it should if I trusted God. Remember that young seminarian whose bicycle handlebars I sat on as we rode and sang songs with my brother Gene? Who would have guessed then that forty-five years later I would be giving a talk about Mother Teresa at his parish, where he was the pastor and my godmother, Aunt Bertha, was a parishioner!

Since then I have traveled all over the world to deliver the message of faith, hope, love, and forgiveness—sometimes speaking to thousands of people at a time. Growing up, I had never once considered doing this. God was writing an unexpected and fascinating chapter in my life.

I continued to wear the special Miraculous Medal that Mother Teresa had given me during my pregnancy with Mary-Catherine. Shortly after Mother Teresa died, I felt inspired to continue her custom of giving blessed Miraculous Medals to people. I felt Mother Teresa was prodding me to do so. I began giving out the medals at my book signings and speaking events, sending them with book orders, and giving them to people I encountered in everyday life.

During one of my trips to Rome, I met with the head of Mother Teresa's archives so that a few of my books and articles about Mother could be reserved there. While at the Missionaries of Charity convent, I spent some quiet time in their chapel. As I prayed, I pondered the words "I thirst" painted on the wall beside the crucifix, and I realized it would take me a lifetime to understand fully what Jesus meant when he said them to the Samaritan woman and again upon the Cross. Yet I knew that our Lord constantly beckons my heart. Next I knelt at Mother Teresa's bed in the simple, unadorned room she used whenever she stayed with her sisters in Rome. Having obtained permission ahead of time, I placed bags of Miraculous Medals upon the blue- and white-checked spread. Resting my folded hands there, I prayed. *Oh, Lord, thank you for bringing me here! Please grant me your many graces.* I also asked dear Mother Teresa for her intercession. Afterward I was given countless opportunities to give away the blessed Miraculous Medals (which I had also placed on Saint John Paul II's tomb).

Because it was known in some Catholic circles that I was devoted to Our Lady of the Miraculous Medal, a publisher asked me to write a book about the history and modern-day stories of the Miraculous Medal. I did and it is titled, *The Miraculous Medal: Stories, Prayers, and Devotions* (Servant Books, 2013).

One of my very first book signings was at a large and well-known bookstore at the Danbury Fair Mall, which stands on the former grounds of the Danbury Fair. It was right before Holy Week, and I was sitting at a table in the doorway of the store—the passersby couldn't miss me. My books were stacked up in neat piles on the table, and I placed a small Mother Teresa prayer card next to them, since I had woven Mother Teresa's inspiration and wisdom throughout the book. Many people came walking by on that busy Saturday afternoon. Some stopped to buy a book and to request my autograph.

One couple was ambling by with a small child sleeping in a stroller. When the man spotted the picture of Mother Teresa he stopped. He lit up and said, "I love Mother Teresa, and I am a Catholic!" He had a need to tell me that and seemed very animated as he moved his tattooed arms expressively. His wife stood beside him, her hands on the stroller. She didn't say anything. I chatted with the man for a few minutes about Mother Teresa, glancing at the woman as well, and I gave them each a Mother Teresa prayer card and blessed Miraculous Medals. We bid our farewells, and they were on their way. Within a couple of minutes the man was back. He seemed out of breath and was very emotional as he explained, "My wife wants a copy of your book!"

"She's over there." He pointed. "She's crying. And she's Jewish!"

It was apparent that the couple had felt overcome with God's amazing grace after receiving the blessed Miraculous Medals. Even though the woman wasn't initially interested in a Catholic book, she suddenly became intrigued. I signed the book for them and commented that the Blessed Mother was Jewish too!

I mentioned earlier that at this same location a horrible violation had happened to me when I was attending the Danbury Fair. It was thirty-five years prior to the book signing at the mall. As I write this book, I am keenly aware that the beautiful occurrence at the bookstore seems to have blossomed from grace born of suffering. Only God knows for sure.

Tears followed me around. At another book signing a woman came to my table. She talked to me but didn't seem interested in purchasing any books. As we chatted, a tear welled up in the corner of her eye and soon tears were streaming down her face and landing on the table. The woman suddenly told me that she just had to have a copy of my book. She asked me to sign one for her.

God's love is powerful! At each and every speaking event, at least one person weeps at some point. At first I was a bit startled because I didn't expect to see people cry, and I was concerned that I was upsetting them. But I soon realized that God was working on their hearts and that the tears were very good indeed. I prayed to be His little instrument doing my best to lead men and women to Him.

As I wrote my books throughout the years, I was blessed with help from my wonderful kids. Joseph and Mary-Catherine have always been supportive. Jessica encouraged me to write this book, *The Kiss of Jesus*, because she said readers need to know more about my life. Chaldea grew to become a very talented artist and has illustrated a few of my books (*Prayerfully Expecting*, *The Heart of Motherhood*, and *The Domestic Church*). Justin has used his talents in technology to help me countless times with computer problems, and with a photograph of the two of us that was used as the cover for *The Heart of Motherhood: Finding Holiness in the Catholic Home* (Crossroad Publishing Company).

The photo originally appeared on Mother's Day on the front page of a newspaper with the caption, "Mothering". A few days before, a photographer had snapped a photo of Justin and me on the swings at a local park. Justin was three years old. I was delighted that with Justin's help the photo could be used again many years later on the cover of my book.

After a while I became a television host on the EWTN television network, sharing encouragement, advice, and the wisdom of the Church. From writing, to speaking, to appearing on radio and television— who would have guessed my winding path would have led me in this direction?

Saying Good-Bye to My Brother

About the time my relationship with EWTN began, I learned that my brother Gary was taken to an emergency room following a seizure. Family members rushed to the hospital to see him. Previously he had been treated for a lung infection, but the doctors wondered if he had been misdiagnosed. After a series of tests they determined that my brother had cancer. He underwent radiation treatments but continued to worsen. The aggressive cancer had metastasized to his brain, where it had caused the seizure. He had more seizures and they worsened. In a very short time Gary was placed in a hospice run by nuns in New York.

I visited as often as I could. Most of the visits were intense because Gary's brain was affected and he would become very worked up about things. When I told him that our brother Gene was coming from Germany to see him, Gary cried out, "It will be too late, it will be too late!" I tried to reassure him and to calm him down, but he was very agitated. I left in tears and wept all the way home. I had never before seen Gary so upset. His words about it being "too late" rang in my ears. Thankfully, Gene wasn't too late. He arrived from Germany soon after and visited with Gary.

Another visit to Gary was less dramatic. I fed Gary his lunch, an unusual experience for me since he was my big brother. He was the third child out of eight, and I was at the end of the family, number seven—the little sister. But I ventured ahead. Suddenly he gagged a bit and spit out what I had fed him. I said, "Oh, I don't blame you. Yuck, mashed peas!" I wiped the food off his face and said, "Don't you worry, I won't give you peas again!" He laughed and laughed.

On my upcoming birthday, there was only one thing I wanted to do. I would go to New York to visit Gary. He had recently slipped into a coma. When I arrived with my husband, Mary-Catherine, and Joseph, Gary seemed to be burning up with fever. I told the nurse, who then administered a fever reducer and loosened his blankets. I wiped my brother's face with a cool washcloth as I silently prayed.

Gary had already received the Anointing of the Sick, yet I felt moved to bless him with the Sign of the Cross using my Brown Scapular. My heart was heavy as I sensed that my big brother would be leaving this world soon, but I needed to recall the real meaning of life. He was going back to the Father, whose Son had suffered and died a cruel death on the Cross so that Gary and every one of us could have eternal life. I kissed my brother good-bye when it was time to head back home to Connecticut. I knew I wouldn't see him again this side of heaven.

The next morning I called the hospice to check on Gary and was told that he had died. It was the day between my birthday and our sister Barbara's birthday and just a few days before his own.

I'll never forget the day of Gary's burial. At first I couldn't find the cemetery and arrived a few minutes late in the pouring rain. I made my way to the grave site and found a few of my relatives standing there. I stared down at a small box covered with a miniature American flag. *My brother is reduced to that*, I thought. I felt sad that this man who had served our country in the Vietnam War was cremated because he had lacked funds for a casket. My tears blended in with the rain drops streaming down my face.

Holy See Invitation amid Challenges

One October day I received a letter from Stanisław Cardinal Rylko, the president of the Pontifical Council for the Laity, inviting me to partic- ipate in an upcoming international conference to mark the twentieth anniversary of Pope John Paul II's Apostolic Letter *Mulieris Dignitatem*. I would be one of 260 delegates from five continents who would travel to the Vatican to consider the theme: "Woman and Man, the *Humanum* in Its Entirety".

The main objectives of the conference, according to the letter of invitation, were

> to review the progress made over the past twenty years in the field of the advancement of women and the recognition of their dignity; to open up a reflection in the light of revelation of the new cultural paradigms and on the difficulties faced by Catholic women as they strive to live according to their identity and to collaborate in fruitful reciprocity with men in building up the Church and society; to remind women of the beauty of the vocation to holiness, that to belong to the Church is to be enfolded in the mystery of communion, and that, as players in the mission of the Church, they are to place all richness of the feminine "genius" at the service of evangelization within the family, in the workplace, politics, and culture.

These were lofty endeavors on the part of the Church, I thought. I was thrilled to have been invited because of the great honor and also because I loved Saint John Paul II, someone I considered to be a hero to women. He had encouraged us to "Be who you are!"

I talked over the invitation with the family and made arrangements to go to Rome. We decided that two of my daughters would accompany me. I would partake in the conference for three days and have a few days to sightsee with the girls. But a week and a half before we were to fly to Italy something happened that threatened to destroy our dream trip.

Mary-Catherine and I were headed back home after shopping and running errands and were just a few miles from our house when a young driver talking on his cell phone slammed into the back of our car. It was the sudden shock of pain in the back of my head and neck that alerted me to the accident. I felt as if I had been hit in the back of the head with a baseball bat. Instead it was the headrest of my seat that had pummeled the back of my head.

I immediately peered over at Mary-Catherine, sitting in the passenger seat, to see if she had experienced the same thing. The look of terror in her eyes answered my question. We had stopped our big SUV at a crosswalk to allow a pedestrian to cross the street. The young man driving the pickup truck was apparently distracted and barreled right into us at high speed.

Trying not to turn my neck too much, I reached over to Mary-Catherine with my right hand and grabbed her left hand. I led us in a short prayer, asking God to take care of us. That was the best I could do, knowing I should not move too much. I felt helpless sitting there, waiting for the ambulance, unable to do more for my daughter.

Clad in neck braces and strapped to body boards, Mary-Catherine and I were taken by ambulance to an emergency room, where we were put in separate rooms. I was in excruciating pain and prayed quietly for my Mary-Catherine and for myself.

After some waiting, a woman came to me and said her seventeen-year-old son was the driver of the truck that hit us. He wanted to talk to me, she said. Then the young man stepped forward. "I'm sorry!" he blurted out as he shed a few tears. He was pretty shaken, realizing what his carelessness had done.

Before I responded to his apology, I asked if I could hold his hand. He switched the coffee to-go cup to his other hand and reached for mine. "It's okay," I said with some tears of my own. "But you need to pray for us, please." I felt compelled to give him some instructions following my forgiveness—it must have been the mom in me. I went on to say that we had no idea what the tests would reveal and would need prayers to heal.

I don't know if anyone had ever told this boy to pray before. He chatted with me for a moment about prayer and promised that he would pray for us. I suspected that the encounter might have been God's way of putting prayer on this young man's mind. In order to drive home another point, the mother in me again felt the need to say something more. "And you need to slow down! You might never have been able to forgive yourself if we had been killed!" I hoped that my simple, earnest words touched him. He nodded his head and said he would slow down. The young man's mother then thanked me for what I said to her son.

Mary-Catherine and I were examined and released that day from the hospital. We were both given medication, and I was also fitted with a cervical collar. The road ahead would be painful, and we were to follow up with our primary doctors and receive physical therapy. As I lay on the love seat in our living room and looked over at Mary-Catherine stretched out on the couch, I had no idea how we would make the trip to Rome. God's grace and the power of prayer would have to get us there. Not being quitters, we rose to the challenge and followed through with our plans for the trip, albeit in pain and uncertainty. We were sure it would be an amazing opportunity that we didn't want to miss.

Going to "The Mountain"

The international congress at the Vatican turned out to be amazing. I was honored to be a part of this history-making event arranged by the Holy See. As one of the chosen delegates seated at the Grand Hotel Palazzo Carpegna near the Vatican, I felt overwhelmed with gratitude. I did not often get the chance to retreat from the world to study, to pray, and to reflect, never mind in Rome. I was filled with joy to be on "the mountain" with the others chosen for this work.

The three days were packed from morning to night with intense, thought-provoking, and affirming conferences, separated by short respites for coffee and meals during which we could converse with fellow participants. Conferences were followed up with open discussions in which delegates in the audience could request opportunities to submit questions to the presenter or the panel. Holy Mass was celebrated each day. In addition to being clad with a translating headset, I also wore my cervical collar to most of the sessions. Throughout the international congress I had the wonderful opportunity to meet many Catholic colleagues and to make new acquaintances too.

Pope John Paul II's Apostolic Letter was written to encourage women in their vocations, to highlight the essential feminine genius that they provide to their families and to the world, and to restore spiritual and physical motherhood to a culture that was quickly losing sight of the dignity of women and mothers. In an era in which the unborn baby might not be safe within his own mother's womb, with debates raging over the nature of marriage, and with confusing messages directed at women about their place in society, the Holy Father's reflections could not have been more timely.

Salvation history depended upon the faithfulness of one young woman in Nazareth and her courageous Yes to the Lord. Throughout history our Church has held women in high esteem, despite what the world might have us think. I deeply believe that women of the third millennium have an amazing opportunity to reap the benefit of the graces being poured out on them now. Women can gain a clearer understanding of their dignity and vocation as they reflect upon Pope John Paul II's affirming and beautiful words for them. I encourage women to read *Mulieris Dignitatem* and to ponder it deeply. Women of our time "can do so much to aid humanity in not falling". It's time to open our hearts to God's message to women and to act upon it. Imbued with the spirit of the gospel, with our Yes we can spread love, understanding, and peace to a world in desperate need.

A highlight of participating in the congress was the audience with Pope Benedict XVI. We delegates were transported to the papal palace, where we excitedly lined up and processed into the meeting room. All 260 of us, representing the various parts of the world, sat together in great anticipation of the Holy Father's address. After thanking us for our work at the congress, Pope Benedict said:

> The question on which you are reflecting has great contemporary relevance: from the second half of the twentieth century until today, the movement for women's rights in the various settings of social life has generated countless reflections and debates, and it has seen the multiplication of many initiatives that the Catholic Church has followed and often accompanied with attentive interest. The male-female relationship, in its respective specificity, reciprocity, and complementarity, without a

doubt constitutes a central point of the "anthropological question" that is so decisive in contemporary culture. The papal interventions and documents that have touched on the emerging reality of the question of women are numerous.... God entrusts to women and to men, according to the characteristics that are proper to each, a specific vocation in the mission of the Church and in the world.

Our audience with the Holy Father was followed by an afternoon of workshops. Cardinal Ryłko then brought the congress to a close and reminded us, "Christ is counting on each of us ... Christ is sending us out." He asked us to remember that the voice and the presence of each of us are important and thanked us for coming together with our contributions. He said the vocation of the lay faithful is to be missionaries and to share our experiences with others. Many of us seemed to be sitting on the edges of our seats and nodding in agreement with him as we accepted our missions, some of us with tears of joy and affirmation in our eyes.

With great enthusiasm, Cardinal Ryłko said, "Come down from the mountain and go against the current—be a contradiction giving witness." He asked us to be unafraid about being a minority. "Salt is a minority but it gives flavor, yeast is a minority but makes the whole dough rise." He also warned us to be careful not to feel invisible, insignificant, or worn out, for Christ has told us that "we are the light of the world and the salt of the earth."

These poignant words resonated in my being—I have used these same words to encourage women through my talks and in my writings. The message renewed my vow to be God's instrument, aiding women to realize their dignity as daughters of God, using the gifts God has given them to help other women struggling in our darkened world. The laity must not be complacent—we all have been given a mission, and by God's grace it will be accomplished through us.

It is my hope that each of us in our various walks of life will study and reflect upon the beautiful Apostolic Letter *Mulieris Dignitatem* of our dear Saint John Paul II and become missionaries to bring the truth about the dignity of women to our confused world. We must not be afraid to be salt and light, leading the way for others, responding with loving hearts, going against the "current" of the culture, and allowing God to minister through us to the wounded around us.

Handicapped Woman on the Street

After the congress concluded I joined my daughters to explore Rome. We had a few days to sightsee before returning home. My favorite place is Saint Peter's Basilica. I never get tired of being right at the heart of our Church.

While exploring Rome my daughters and I decided to visit a few street markets and areas off the beaten path. Chaldea was looking at a few artsy things, and Mary-Catherine and I decided to venture around the corner. Unexpectedly we came upon an old crippled woman who was sitting on the street next to a garbage dumpster. Her legs were outstretched and her crutches lay beside her. I couldn't help but notice the many tumor-like protrusions poking up from all over her head through her sparse wisps of white hair.

Her head was bowed down a bit due to what may have been spinal and neck troubles. Tears started to flow from my eyes, and I quickly wiped them away. I approached the woman and began talking to her. She nodded at me, but I really didn't know if she understood my English. I didn't know what language she spoke because she didn't utter a word. I felt quite emotional during this encounter. I wanted to do something to protect the woman from the street and from her life of apparent poverty and pain. Perhaps the fact that I was unable to change her plight caused me further torment. My heart was full of love for this woman.

Mary-Catherine saw my tears and knew I wanted to help in some way. She asked if I had a Miraculous Medal I could give her. I felt certain I didn't bring any with me for that outing because I had packed lightly. But as I reached into my pocket I found a large Miraculous Medal that had been blessed by Pope Benedict XVI at the audience the previous day. I reached out and handed it to the woman. As I did, I pointed to the medal and said, "There's Mary!" The woman nodded and seemed to understand what I meant. Instead of placing it in her tin can of money, she placed it in her pocket. I had to continue to wipe tears from my eyes because I didn't want to make a scene with my emotions.

I had no idea if she would understand me, but I asked her if we could say a prayer together. She nodded. I began with the Sign of the Cross and so did she. I said the words of the Our Father out loud and moved on to the Hail Mary. The woman was mumbling quietly along. I knew that she was praying too. We finished with the Sign of the Cross. She picked her head up for the first time from the drooped position and looked straight into my eyes. As she gazed into my eyes I took her hands in mine and began kissing them all over. I then cradled her face with my hands and felt so much love for her that I knew in my heart she was Jesus in the distressing disguise of the poorest of the poor, as Mother Teresa would say. Mother's motto "Love is the reason for my life" echoed in my heart. The woman wiped her tears with a tissue, and I traced a cross on her forehead lightly with my thumb. I didn't want to leave this woman, so I stood there for awhile before bidding her good-bye.

Panic Attacks, Another Kind of Pain

The girls and I flew back to the United States and tried our best to settle into a regular routine. For Mary-Catherine and me it would mean going to physical therapy three times a week as well as to the doctor and neurologist. Our backs and necks had been traumatized from the car accident. The doctors also discovered that we had both sustained brain injuries. A brain injury is sometimes referred to as the "invisible injury" because the patient appears fine to others but in reality suffers in many ways neurologically.

It would be a couple of years of physical therapy before our necks and backs would heal, and even then we were both left with permanent damage. I hoped and prayed that our talk in the hospital might have had some sort of impact on the young driver's life. I also hoped that perhaps because we were stopped at the crosswalk, we protected the woman who was crossing the street from being killed by the speeding truck. Only God knows this for sure.

Part of my suffering was the onset of panic attacks, which recurred for almost two years after the car accident. Before the brain injury, I had never experienced a panic attack, which is an intense feeling of crippling fear. There's no rhyme or reason to it. The feeling of panic has nothing to do with being afraid of something. The only thing I can compare a panic attack to is the "impending doom" feeling that I had experienced a few times with an allergic reaction to a medication. There's nothing that can be done about a panic attack but to endure it by believing it will eventually end. As awful as these panic attacks were, I am actually glad I experienced them so that I can empathize with someone going through one. I am also thankful that I am no longer plagued with them.

Mother Teresa in My Heart

Mother Teresa's love and wisdom remain with me. I believe that her prayers and guidance while she was alive and in touch with me have greatly aided me on my spiritual journey, and that her prayers and assistance from heaven have helped me too.

Mother Teresa often spoke of "Jesus in the distressing disguise of the poorest of the poor". Her work with the poor and the dying brought her face to face with countless people in dreadful, extreme, and urgent situations. Yet Mother Teresa was very outspoken about another kind of poverty too. She often said that affluent countries, especially the United States, suffer from the poverty of loneliness and the hunger for love. The Missionaries of Charity follow Jesus' words: "Whatever you do to the least of my brothers, you do to me." They believe that when they care for those God puts in their midst, they are truly serving Jesus Himself.

One day as I was praying I heard a clear message rising up from within me, "Your vocation is to love." I got right down on my knees and wept. I could just about *feel* the love God was pouring into my heart, love that He wanted me to share with others.

So many people are wounded by family problems, broken relationships, abandonment, abuse, and pain. Whenever I travel I encounter people bearing deep scars, and my vocation to love, which began within my own family, has led to many opportunities to reach out to hurting strangers with the love of God.

Pope Francis said, "I say to myself, and I say to you: Do we let God write our lives? Or do we want to do the writing ourselves? Do you have the capacity to find the word of God in the story of each day? Or are your ideas the ones that you hold up and you do not let the surprises of the Lord speak to you?" (Homily, October 7, 2013). We let God "write our lives" by giving ourselves to Him each day. The gift of ourselves begins first thing in the morning, when we pray that God will use us this day for His glory. He works in powerful ways through ordinary occurrences.

With all of the people we meet in the course of our daily lives, we are to be the "aroma" of Christ.

But thanks be to God, who in Christ always leads us in triumph, and through us spreads the fragrance of the knowledge of him everywhere. For we are the aroma of Christ to God among those who are being saved

and among those who are perishing . . . For we are not, like so many, ped-
dlers of God's word; but as men of sincerity, as commissioned by God, in
the sight of God we speak in Christ. (2 Cor 2:14–17)

Saint Paul uses the analogy of incense to remind us of who we are in the
world. We are to be the sweet fragrance of Christ, who for our sakes
offered His life to the Father. By being faithful to Christ, we can't help
but lead others toward heaven. We need to be mindful that all we do
and say can have an effect on others.

Once on a very bumpy flight back to the United States from Rome,
I sat across from a twenty-something young woman who was visibly
frightened by the turbulence. I instinctively reached out to touch her
arm and to tell her not to worry. I also offered her my rosary beads to
hold. She gladly accepted the beads and drew them to her heart. I also
gave her a blessed Miraculous Medal, which she added to the long fashionable chain she was wearing. The medal was one that Blessed Mother
Teresa had given to me. We had a nice conversation throughout our
journey, and I reassured her that I was praying. She thanked me profusely and gave me a big hug when we finally landed in New York.

I was happy to have helped the young woman by offering prayers
and comfort, as well as the blessed objects, which are sacramentals. I will
never know the full impact that these gifts had on her life. Perhaps they
nudged her to pray more. Maybe they made her think of Mother Mary.
I don't know. But a very interesting thing happened after I reached out
to the girl. Sometime into the flight I received a tap on my arm from
behind. I turned to see an elderly man leaning toward me from a couple
of rows back.

"How did you do that?" he asked me.

I wondered what he meant and hesitated.

"The girl—you helped her. How did you do that?"

I had never been asked a question like this before. To me, I had only
done what came naturally. Apparently, my simple act of love moved this
man in some way. At least it got him thinking. It even prodded him to
tap me on the arm and ask a question.

"Well," I answered, "God must have put a lot of love in my heart. I
like to help people." As simple as that—the unadorned explanation just
came out. It satisfied the man. And I was able to get the word "God"
in there—something for the man to think about. He wiped a few tears

from his eyes. We are the aroma of Christ whenever we share with others the love He has shared with us.

One day when Mary-Catherine was about three years old, she wanted to wear a pretty dress to the school bus stop. As usual we were in a rush to get her siblings to the bus stop, so I didn't argue about her fashion choice. Nor did I really mind; I liked her to dress femininely. I helped her into her frilly frock and off we went to the bus stop. We bid her older siblings good-bye, and then my neighbor Beatrice (not her real name) complimented Mary-Catherine on her dress.

"It's really her church dress but she insisted on wearing it today," I explained.

Suddenly a few tears trickled down Beatrice's face. Almost immediately she started to sob. I was puzzled as to why she was so upset. We had been talking about a dress. She then revealed to me the promise she had made to her father eight years prior. She said while her father was on his death bed he pleaded for her to get her baby son baptized. Beatrice promised that she would do so but never followed through.

As she poured out the details, she sobbed away. I offered her a hug, which she gladly accepted. And it finally dawned on me why she recalled her promise to her father that ordinary morning—the word "church". That one word brought the distant memory to the forefront of Beatrice's mind, and she felt deep remorse for not having fulfilled her promise to her dying father. What's more, she now felt as if it were too late. Her son was eight years old.

"Of course it's not too late," I said reassuringly.

"But they'll laugh at me—they'll yell at me," she said, and then she cried some more.

After a little more conversation I was able to convince Beatrice that she and her son would not be scorned but would be welcomed with open arms. I offered to call our pastor on her behalf to arrange for the Baptism. She accepted, and before long her son was baptized. But the story does not end there. Beatrice went to confession and came back into the graces of the Church. Her boy went to faith formation classes to receive First Reconciliation and First Holy Communion, and Beatrice helped out in the faith formation office while he was at his classes. All this grace was put into motion because of that word "church". I am exceedingly thankful that because of God's amazing grace, my daughter and I were instrumental in helping this family on their journey toward heaven.

God's Great Mercy

I have been in touch with Chris' mother, Elizabeth, for a number of years. We reconnected unexpectedly when Elizabeth called my home phone number by mistake to inquire about an art exhibit Chaldea would be hosting. She saw the phone number in a newspaper article about the art show and thought she was calling the art studio. We ended up talking for over an hour on the phone and made plans to get together. We have been visiting with one another and staying in touch by phone ever since. She still refers to me as her daughter-in-law. This relationship with my former mother-in-law might seem strange, but God's ways are amazing.

Elizabeth told me one day that her other son, Paul (not his real name), was in the hospital with cancer. He had been having unexplained pain and weight loss for a while and finally had it checked out. I hadn't seen or spoken with Paul in about twenty-five years, but when I heard he was hospitalized I arranged to go with his mother to visit him. Paul was happy to see me and asked me to stay in touch, and I visited him as often as I could, bringing homemade chicken soup and oatmeal cookies. I also called Paul on the phone frequently.

Paul's cancer was very aggressive, and I was saddened to see a once-strong man begin to wither away so rapidly. Thinking Paul wouldn't live much longer, I knew that I needed to broach the subject of prayer with him, even though we had never talked about it before. There wasn't anyone in his family who would be concerned for his spiritual well-being because they were all nonbelievers. Knowing it might be awkward to mention God, I prayed for His guidance and will.

One day I told Paul that I had been praying for him. During subsequent visits I ventured a bit more, expanding our spiritual discussions. I gently explained that he should prepare his heart and his soul for when he would meet God, and he told me that he had begun to pray—mostly for others.

I am very thankful that I spoke up about prayer when I did because soon afterward Paul fell into a coma. During one of my visits to Paul, I looked up at the clock and noticed it was about 2:40 P.M. I took out my rosary beads and began to pray the Divine Mercy Chaplet. Jesus had asked Saint Faustina to pray the Divine Mercy Chaplet especially for sinners and the dying, as quoted in her *Diary*:

Pray as much as you can for the dying. By your entreaties obtain for them trust in My mercy, because they have most need of trust, and have it the least. Be assured that the grace of eternal salvation for certain souls in their final moments depends on your prayer. You know the whole abyss of My mercy, so draw upon it for yourself and especially for poor sinners. Sooner would heaven and earth turn into nothingness than would My mercy not embrace a trusting soul. (1777)

Jesus also told Saint Faustina:

My daughter, encourage souls to say the chaplet which I have given you. It pleases Me to grant everything they ask of Me by saying the chaplet.... Write that when they say this chaplet in the presence of the dying, I will stand between My Father and the dying person, not as the just Judge but as the merciful Savior. (1541)

I finished praying the chaplet for Paul at just about 3:00 P.M., the Hour of Great Mercy. I had a very strong urge to baptize him. For a while I had been thinking that I should and had been waiting for the right moment to unfold. Paul was not a Catholic, and the family had no desire to call a priest to visit with him. But I knew that Paul wanted to go to heaven. In Paul's dire need, right when he would be leaving his earthly life, I knew I needed to step in and to baptize him right there in his hospital bed.

I pulled out the holy water that I had been carrying in my purse, awaiting the proper time to baptize Paul. I whispered another prayer, looked toward the door to see if anyone was approaching, and proceeded to baptize Paul into the Church, pouring the holy water over his forehead three times while pronouncing the words of Baptism. Paul, who had been totally silent for the entire visit and for days before that, let out a groan from the depths of his being with each gentle pouring of the holy water—at each utterance of the baptismal formula.

I stayed with Paul for a little while longer. Before leaving his hospital room I leaned over and gave him a kiss good-bye. I was certain that I wouldn't see Paul again on this side of heaven. A few hours later I received a phone call from his mother telling me that Paul had died a couple of hours after my visit.

One year to the day after Paul died happened to be the Feast of the Visitation commemorating the Blessed Mother Mary's visit to Saint

Elizabeth, and I found myself going "in haste" to visit his still-grieving mother on the first anniversary of her grown son's untimely death. I didn't realize until later that the person I was visiting on this feast day was aptly named Elizabeth, not that I am comparing myself to the Blessed Mother! I am only her little daughter, trying to emulate her virtues.

I told Elizabeth that I would like to take her out to lunch if she would like to go. I wanted to get her out of her little apartment and hoped it would help to alleviate some of her emotional pain. She welcomed the diversion and the company too, since she lived alone. On the way to the restaurant, we passed a Catholic church, and Elizabeth suddenly pointed out that she had been baptized there as a baby. Prior to that announcement I hadn't a clue that she was a baptized Catholic, because during the many years I had known her she had been an atheist. Since she brought up the subject of Baptism, I felt very comfortable asking her a question—one I had pondered for the past year but didn't dare mention since Elizabeth had been grieving intensely: "Did you have Paul baptized?"

"No, honey, I didn't."

My heart secretly soared because I wholeheartedly believed that Paul went straight to heaven, having received his one and only Baptism moments before his death! It was no coincidence that Elizabeth and I should *happen* to pass by the church where Elizabeth was baptized and that I had the opportunity to ask her about Paul. God's ways are mysterious. I could never have imagined many years ago, when Chris and I divorced, that one day God would use me to bring his brother into the Church in his final hours—especially since Paul was one of the many relatives from Chris' family who had gathered at the courthouse during my divorce from Charlie.

Another relative at the courthouse that day was Chris' aunt Dolores (not her real name). When she was dying, I visited her and blessed her with my Brown Scapular, but that was not the last of God's grace in our relationship. After Paul's death, I helped Elizabeth to sort through his belongings. They were in a storage shed along with some of Dolores' things, and everything had to be moved by a certain deadline. Most of the items we tossed into a dumpster, but we found some photographs and other little treasures that I encouraged Elizabeth to keep. As I rummaged through the stuff, I came upon a tiny jewelry box. I opened it to discover a familiar item that I hadn't seen in almost thirty years: the cross that Dolores had given to Chaldea as a baptismal gift and then taken back after the divorce. It had collected dust in the storage unit after Dolores had died. As surprised and happy as I was to be holding it again, I felt sadness too. I shook my head over the senselessness of it, of the pain in the family that perhaps motivated Dolores to take back the gift. Finding the cross seemed to be a sign of God's mysterious presence in all of our lives, even in the darkest corners. I rescued the cross from being thrown into the dumpster and brought it home.

Chicken Soup Evangelization

Ellen (not her real name), my elderly neighbor, is an atheist. She's a good person who cannot understand how a God can exist when there is evil in the world. Ellen lives alone and is a shut-in due to disabilities, so I started to call her on the phone and once in a while stop in to see her. One day Ellen told me she didn't want me to preach to her. One of her friends had been doing that, she said, and she felt the need to tell me not to. I promised I would respect her request.

I resolved to keep in touch with Ellen with kind phone calls and visits, and whenever I could I would bring her homemade chicken soup. I wanted to cheer her up because she felt lonely quite often due to her health-related limitations and her inability to get out of her little bungalow. Ellen always appreciated my visits and calls.

One day as I headed over to see Ellen I prayed that God would shine right through me to reach her. I was greeted at the door by Ellen's home health aide, who suddenly recognized me from a book signing a couple of years ago. Ellen invited the aide to sit down with us. Our conversation turned to my books and my speaking engagements, and my appearances on television and radio. Normally, Ellen didn't want to talk about God, but this time she was clearly intrigued. She asked me how I got involved in these activities in the first place. We had a very beautiful exchange, and when it was time for me to leave Ellen did something totally out of character. After a warm good-bye hug, she took my two hands in hers said, "Donna, please don't ever stop praying for me."

Ellen was attracted to the love of Jesus. She clearly did not want someone preaching at her, but she accepted Jesus' love. His love transforms our hearts and souls and draws us to Him. It's essential that we pray and ask God to use us to bring others to Him and then allow Him to do it in His way, which is all about love. Christ's love is miraculous!

Ellen and I have since enjoyed many conversations about God. One time Ellen told me she was very concerned and saddened about terrible things going on in the world. She said she just didn't know what to do about them. I responded by telling her that I pray about those things and give them to God to take care of, and then I can feel peace. Ellen seemed to find comfort in my response and said that she would pray too. I find it heartening that an atheist is now praying. God's ways are amazing.

Fighting for My Life

Father Hardon had taught theology with a passion. He knew what was at the heart of our faith and tried to explain it in his talks and in his books. He said, "To be a true Christian means to expect the cross. To be a true Christian means not to run away from the cross." He encouraged us to ponder the lives of the saints who came to understand the mystery of the cross. He said, "It means to recognize what those who suffered before us to pass on the faith to us realized: that in the cross is salvation; in the cross is life; in the cross is strength of mind; in the cross is joy of spirit; in the cross is height of virtue."

But there's one more critical element. Father Hardon explained, "All of this is true, as the passages of the Gospels make eloquently plain. But on one condition. The cross and suffering and crucifixion—Christ's and ours—have only as much meaning as we have faith and love" (*Spiritual Life in the Modern World*).

I felt very connected to Jesus' Passion and death on the Cross. By God's grace, I knew that Christ did His finest work when He allowed Himself to be nailed to the Cross for our sakes. So when the attending nurse said to me, "Well, it's not as if nails are being driven into the palms of your hands," I nearly fell off my chair! Allow me to back up a bit to explain.

I had been dealing with some stubborn urinary tract infections, and one night I awoke to find my heart racing and my body burning up with a fever. I was in a lot of pain too, and when I went to the bathroom I discovered that my urine was bloody! I called my doctor, and he told me to go to the hospital. I was feeling a bit delirious and was thankful that Dave could drive me there. A CAT scan determined the site of the infection, and I was given strong antibiotics. Then I was released to go home and rest.

When I followed up with my urologist, I noticed that he and his staff were making mistakes. For instance, they tried to put me on a medication to which I was allergic. Another time they failed to send a urine sample to the lab for results needed to determine treatment. I never would have had the serious problem that sent me to the emergency room in the middle of the night had they done things properly. I therefore decided to seek another urologist.

The new doctor ordered a battery of tests, and I already felt I was in better hands. Around eight o'clock that night the doctor called to say that bacteria different from that already being treated had been found in my urinary tract. He said that the infection was serious and that he had already made arrangements for me to visit an infusion center the following morning.

After his call I researched the bacteria and discovered that it can be fatal, if the infection spreads to other parts of the body. I recalled the young Brazilian model I had read about in the news several months prior. The poor woman had her hands and feet amputated and still she died from the same bacteria I now had. I became frightened, and I had trouble sleeping that night. The next morning I grabbed a light jacket since it was a bit chilly that day and happily, I discovered a rosary in the pocket. It was one with a relic of Saint Thérèse of Lisieux, which I had misplaced.

Before Dave drove me to the hospital, I called my sister Barbara and asked her to pray for me. I was feeling a bit overwhelmed, and Barbara gave me some warm words of encouragement and promised her prayers. I was thankful for her support and the fact that my husband would be with me.

Before I could receive the medication at the infusion center, I had to sign papers stating that I wouldn't sue the hospital if I lost my hearing or if my kidneys shut down. These were two of the potential side effects to this very strong medication, which was the only one that I could tolerate that would be effective. Needless to say, this discovery added to my anxiety.

My nurse, Paula (not her real name), attempted three times to insert the IV in my left arm, and each time she gave me an injection that sent a burning, stinging pain up my arm. Discretely holding my rosary in my right hand, I prayed silently. Since Holy Week was fast approaching,

Jesus' Passion and death were at the forefront of my mind, and I prayed that the suffering I was enduring might be united with His. I prayed that any graces I might be able to receive could be redemptive and useful for souls who needed it, maybe even for my nurse who was caring for me. I also prayed that I not have an adverse reaction to the medicine and that it heal my infection. Believing that Jesus knew what was best for my soul, I placed my trust in Him—whatever would happen.

As I was praying Paula said matter-of-factly, "No offering it up, here."
What? How can she know what I am thinking and praying?
"It's not as if nails are being driven into the palms of your hands."
"Well, yes, I am offering it up," I said.
That broke the ice.

We chatted after Paula successfully got the IV in place and started the medication. I asked her if I would be able to make a trip to Pennsylvania in about a week. She said that I would have to ask the doctor, but she doubted it because I was scheduled for ten days of infusion therapy. Then she asked why I wanted to go to Pennsylvania. I said I had a speaking event scheduled and didn't want to disappoint the women's group. One thing led to another, and I explained that I was a Catholic author.

"Oh, I am a Catholic too, but not a very good one," she confessed.

I eventually asked if I could bring her one of my books as a gift the following day. She seemed delighted, so I did and signed it for her. She then said she wanted to see all of my books. The next day I brought her a copy of each one, and she took them all.

During my remaining visits to the infusion center, we chatted about the faith. On the last day of my therapy, Paula gave me a big good-bye hug in the middle of the room.

"Donna, you came into my life just when I needed you most," she said, and I had no doubt that God had used my bit of suffering to touch Paula's heart in some way. Jesus had always been in Paula's life, but now she could respond to "Jesus with skin", meaning me, a flesh-and-blood human being who had brought her the love of Jesus. We all have opportunities every day to be "Jesus with skin" to others.

A Dish of Rice

Blessed Mother Teresa said that it is far easier to serve a dish of rice to a starving person on the other side of the world than it is to serve that dish of rice to someone in our own home who is starving for love. Serving that person on the other side of the world may consist in writing out a check or even in traveling far distances to help the unfortunate. But it's often a lot more difficult for us to show our love to those nearest to us—a teenager who is acting up, a toddler running circles around everyone, or a spouse who is difficult or grouchy. We must look around our own homes to see if there is someone in need of God's love. Sharing God's love begins there. We might be misguided or confused, thinking we need to spread our love elsewhere and to join various organizations in an attempt to do so. Or we may be afraid to bare our hearts and souls to the ones we love. As much as we may want to run away at times from those needing love under our own roof, we would be wrong to neglect our duties at home in order to serve others elsewhere.

First, let us be sure to serve that "dish of rice" to our loved ones at home in the family. Then if God gives us a surplus of time and energy we can roll up our sleeves and serve those beyond our family. My point is that we need to pause and to search our hearts to be sure we are taking proper care of those whom God has entrusted to us. God is counting on us to serve Him in those He surrounds us with. Let us be sure to get our priorities straight.

The irritable, the angst-ridden, and the contradictory—those family members and neighbors who challenge us in some way—actually help us on our way to heaven. We need to ask God for grace and an extra dose of faith, hope, and charity to be able to love the very people God wants us to serve. We are actually called to love them into heaven! In the course of even just one day, God gives us many opportunities to act on grace, to love our family members and others near us, to set an example by our selfless service to them. It's not always easy; in fact, most times it is very difficult.

Sometimes the little loving details seem, well, little. However, I am convinced that when we pray throughout our little details of loving service, these acts of love are really huge in God's eyes. He works through them all and sanctifies them. So, let's be sure not to neglect the opportunities around us to live in our present moments of life, opening our hearts to those God puts in our midst.

Onward with Love

People are hungry for God. People are hungry for love.... Do you have eyes to see? Quite often we look but we don't see. We are all passing through this world. We need to open our eyes and see.

—Mother Teresa

Mother Teresa often spoke about those who are unwanted, fearful, and unloved, or who have been rejected by society. She said such a "person experiences a kind of poverty that is much more painful and deep" than the starving people whose hunger can be satisfied with food (*One Heart Full of Love*). She said, "The cure is much more difficult to find" for those who are abandoned and unloved. Mother Teresa believed that these people share in the Passion of Christ, which "is being lived everywhere". She asks us, "Are we willing to share in this passion? Are we willing to share people's sufferings?"

The Mother in Me

My vocation to motherhood is extremely important to me. I am mother to my biological children, but I am also a spiritual mother to others. God calls us to care for others, and in my case (and that of other women) that means to "mother" them. We are all asked to leave our comfort zones and to help those in need who are near to us and in some cases those who are far away. Mother Teresa was an exceptional example of spiritual motherhood.

As I was flying home from Alabama, where I did some television shows on EWTN, I sat next to a woman named Joan. She and I got into a spiritual discussion (as often happens with me on flights!), and Joan explained that she had some trouble with the Church. I felt inspired to give her a blessed Miraculous Medal that I had in my pocket, and she held it in her hand as we chatted for more than two hours. By the time we reached our layover destination, Joan was beaming and thanking me for the medal and the conversation. She said she had no doubt that it was meant to be that we sat next to each other. Of course, I have no doubt either. I have experienced many transforming encounters throughout my travels, and I always pray that God will work His miracles in the hearts of those I meet.

Joan and I decided to spend some time together while we waited for our next flight. While Joan was scouting out a tram to ride to the other end of the airport, I spotted a young mother having a complete meltdown. She was sitting on the floor in the middle of the corridor, crying and yelling at her two small children, one of which was in a stroller. For some reason the baby looked very familiar. With her belongings scattered around her, she was frantically searching through a piece of luggage for something. Since she looked so distraught I thought I could possibly lend a hand. I knelt down beside her and the children so that I could be at their level and asked if I could help. The stressed-out young woman took a puff on her inhaler and blurted out that she was sure she had left her cell phone on the plane and that she needed to make a call. I let her use my cell phone to call her own because it might be in her bag. She did, and it was indeed in her bag.

A conversation unfolded between us. April was her name, and she proceeded to pour out her woes. Through tears she told me that she was in the process of a divorce and on her way to California to bring the children to their father. In addition, her fourteen-year-old sister was pregnant. April caught her breath and took another puff on her inhaler, and I asked if I could give her a hug. She accepted, and as I embraced her she hugged me tightly back. She sighed, shed a few more tears, and then she told me that she had been abandoned by both her mother and her stepmother. She really had needed that mother's hug.

I pulled out a blessed Miraculous Medal and pointed to Mary on the medal. "Look, here is Mary, *she* is your Mother! She'll teach you how to mother your children." Then I gave her the medal. She said she was Catholic and sighed again. It seemed as if the mention of the Blessed Mother had touched April's heart.

Joan found her way back to where April and I were, and she offered the young mother help as well. I felt very blessed to be part of what God had arranged. During the entire encounter, April's young son in the stroller was watching intently. He never took his eyes off me. There was something powerful about his gaze. It wasn't until later, when reflecting upon the event, that I realized something incredible. The day prior to the airport encounter I had looked intently at a painting hanging at EWTN. As the cameraman Mike and I stood before the painting, waiting for the set to be arranged, Mike mentioned that the eyes of Baby Jesus in Mary's arms were penetrating and beautiful. He marveled over how the artist had depicted them—"almost like adult eyes in a baby's face". Then it hit me. In addition to the many blessings occurring in my encounter with April, it seemed as though Jesus was watching me through her baby's eyes.

"Homeless" in Rome

Once while in Rome for a conference, I experienced something very remarkable: I felt what it is like to be homeless. I had arranged to arrive in Rome on September 5, Mother Teresa's feast day, and to attend with the Missionaries of Charity a Mass and ceremony in her honor.

After flying all night and not sleeping even one wink on the plane, I arrived in Rome exhausted. I got a ride from the airport to my friend's apartment, where I would be staying for the week while my friend was out of town. But since it was Sunday the doorman was not there, which meant I couldn't get the key to the apartment. Standing on the cobblestone sidewalk with an embarrassingly huge suitcase (at the time I owned a small one and a large one, but nothing in between), I asked the driver what I should do. He offered to take me to the Missionaries of Charity, since I had mentioned that I would be seeing them later in the day, and this seemed like a good idea, because I had no place else to go with that gigantic suitcase.

The Missionaries of Charity invited me in and escorted me to their women's shelter, where they had an extra bed, and suggested I rest for a while. I really couldn't settle my brain yet, because I had loose ends to think about, and tried several times to get in touch with my friend and my family, but to no avail. The phone at the convent was not working.

Eventually, I did stretch out on the bed, and I felt very alone. The sisters were resting, and the guests were out in the courtyard smoking and talking. Lack of sleep, aches and pains from traveling, being in a country where I didn't speak the language, and not knowing what to do or where to go accentuated my feeling of aloneness. But, it was also more than that. I was feeling overwhelmingly homeless and displaced in a very profound way. I couldn't shake the feeling.

I ended up taking a quick shower in the shelter using shampoo and even a towel from one of the women there who assured me the towel had just come out of the clean laundry. The towel was very small, tattered and quite stiff, but I was thankful for it for a couple of reasons—for drying myself and for being more grateful for the towels I am fortunate to own back home.

I was served a simple lunch in the shelter, and I sat across the picnic-style table from a young woman who was apparently mentally handicapped. As we chatted, I saw Jesus in her eyes. Then I was off to the chapel decorated in Mother Teresa's honor. After the Mass, I was transported to another part of Rome, to the other Missionaries of Charity convent. The small car sped through tiny streets while a mother held her child on her lap and her husband drove hurriedly. I wondered why their little child was not in a car seat. They spoke no English, and the mother smiled at me as I tried to communicate with them. Eventually, I gave up trying since they didn't understand a word I said nor did I understand them. The smiles between us were good enough, I concluded.

Upon arriving I had to drag my enormous suitcase up about a million stone steps. I'm exaggerating, of course. But, I wish I had counted those steps—there were so many. I was under the impression that I would be staying with the sisters or somewhere near them. I just needed a place for the night and planned to return to my friend's home for the key the following day.

I arrived just in time for another special Mass for Mother Teresa, which was extremely crowded. Many times during the liturgy I felt my eyes misting with tears and felt God's grace working in my heart.

Afterward I learned that I had misunderstood what I had been told before. I would not be spending the night there because there wasn't a women's shelter at this convent, only one for men. A sister said that she would look for someplace else I could stay, and I trusted that God had a plan.

A couple whom Sister knew offered to take me in for the night and to drive me to my friend's apartment the following day. We stopped to get a pizza to bring home for dinner, and we had a lovely conversation around their modest kitchen table, even though the family spoke very little English and I spoke no Italian. Later, as I pulled the blanket over me on their trundle bed, I counted my blessings and felt amazed at God's interesting plans. I could feel Christ's love enveloping me after that odd adventure of feeling displaced.

The following night, after getting settled into my friend's apartment, my heart began racing. It does this sometimes, especially when I haven't gotten enough sleep, because of an electrical heart problem I developed during my pregnancy with Joseph. I did a few of the things that sometimes restore its regular rhythm, but nothing worked. I called my new friends on the phone, and though they didn't speak much English, the couple and their adult daughter came over to the apartment right away. When they arrived they called their doctor, who spoke English. She encouraged me to get examined at the hospital. I decided to see if I got better on my own first, before going through the ordeal of visiting an Italian hospital. My new friends made me a cup of chamomile tea, and I rested; and thank God I did get better. Since the encounter years ago with this gracious Italian couple and their family, we have kept in touch.

After this fascinating yet perplexing adventure, I returned to the first Missionaries of Charity convent where the mother superior expressed something quite extraordinary. She said exuberantly, "Oh, Donna-Marie! Our Lord brought you here to us on Mother Teresa's feast day so that you could feel homeless!" I hadn't told her about my interior trial, yet she went on to describe the beauty of knowing and understanding how Jesus often felt and how His poor often feel. She reassured me that Mother Teresa was watching over me. It was a profound experience that moved me to thankful tears.

Losing My Sister, My "Other Mother"

My sister Barbara called me one day from an intensive care unit. She had been rushed there by ambulance, and tests were being administered as we spoke. Her doctors feared something serious. Barbara had previously beat lung cancer, and we had been counting our blessings. *Now what?* I knew in my heart that I had better act quickly. In addition to offering urgent prayers, I started looking into flights to Texas. As I tied up loose ends at home and prepared to go to Barbara, she received the news that she had acute leukemia. She was told she might have only a few months to live. Barbara was transported to her home to receive hospice care. When I spoke to her on the phone, she said, "I'm not giving up, Donna."

Many people were praying by now. I flew to Texas a few days after we spoke, and I brought with me a relic of Blessed Mother Teresa that was given to me for my sister by the Missionaries of Charity. The kind nun told me over the phone that she and the other sisters would be praying for Barbara and the family. She also blessed me over the phone and in a letter with some beautiful, poignant words from Mother Teresa to take to my heart: "Death is nothing except going back to God, where He is and where we belong.... Death is the most decisive moment in human life. It is like our Coronation: to die in peace with God."

At Barbara's request, I put the special blessed Miraculous Medal I brought to her on the chain around her neck. It was one of many medals I had placed on Saint John Paul II's tomb and Blessed Mother Teresa's bed in Rome. During the first few days I was at my sister's home, we conversed between her many naps. When she slept I quietly prayed the Rosary and the Divine Mercy Chaplet. Much of the time I couldn't concentrate on my prayers; I was constantly repeating them or starting over when I lost my place. I knew that God didn't mind if I couldn't get it just right; He understood that I was distraught. His concern was where my heart was, not necessarily my mind.

Mother Teresa had said, "When the time comes and we cannot pray, it is very simple—let Jesus pray in us to the Father in the silence of our hearts. If we cannot speak, He will speak. If we cannot pray, He will pray. So let us give Him our inability and our nothingness" (*Love: A Fruit Always in Season*).

I made healthy frozen fruit and yogurt smoothies for Barbara, which she sipped from a straw, and I planned to bake her some fresh banana bread too, because it was something she said she would enjoy. I filled my sister in on family news, held her hand, stroked her arm, kissed and hugged her, and told her that I loved her with all my heart. We talked about serious matters and stupid stuff too—at times acting as if no one was actually dying. I told her I liked her pretty curtains; she said she wanted her sparse hair to grow in to be like my hairstyle. I choked back tears because I doubted there would be time for that. All the while we both treasured being together. Barbara told me she wished that God could come down with a time stamp and declare just how much time she had left.

"Is it a couple of weeks, six months, or a year?" she asked. It all happened too fast for anyone to comprehend.

Barbara's children, grandchildren, family members, and nurses came in and out to care for her and to visit, spending precious time—that *thing* we were curious about. Time—how much was left? Our sister Alice Jean, her husband, Luis, and their son Kenneth came often to visit. Barbara's daughter Donna Jean stayed around the clock. Her daughter Allison visited often. Barbara's little dog, Cricket, lay faithfully alongside her, sensing her need for comfort and companionship.

We were planning to watch a family video together at some point. That never happened. I never did bake that banana bread either. There just wasn't enough time. Barbara's illness was racing ahead like a runaway freight train. Yet she struggled to keep her eyes open, saying she didn't want to miss anything.

One day I sensed I should expedite a request to Barbara's friend, a priest, to arrange for the Anointing of the Sick. She had been anointed earlier at the hospital, but I wanted her to have the sacrament again, now that she was fast approaching her death. Monsignor, who had administered the sacrament at the hospital, asked if she was in a critical state and I confirmed that she was. He came straight away from the hospital after my call. When he walked through the door, I was amazed that Barbara suddenly sat up from her slumber and became very alert for the sacrament she was about to receive. Barbara's daughters and I knelt around her bed while the monsignor anointed her. Her breathing improved, and she seemed more content—she was calm.

Monsignor requested that the family call immediately for the parish priest to bring Viaticum—Holy Communion as "food for the journey" home to heaven. Her daughter Allison took care of that. The priest came quickly, and after he said a few prayers he placed a small piece of the blessed Host on Barbara's tongue. She was able to take it. A visible peace came over her whole countenance and then she rested. Her son George arrived from Houston. Now all of her children were around her. We kept a quiet yet unwavering vigil over our loved one, watching her breathe, administering medicine, and giving her gentle caresses and love.

The following day, Barbara passed to her eternal reward. It was really difficult to fathom how fast my sister's death had come. She was supposed to have a few months left, according to her doctors, but she had only five days after I arrived at her apartment. I feel blessed having gone to Texas as quickly as I did. Had I waited even a few more days (as I had previously considered), I wouldn't have been able to talk with Barbara.

As sorrowful as it was for me to watch my sister suffer and wither away in her last days, I felt a great deal of peace in my heart knowing that Barbara, whom I considered to be my "second mother", was on her way home to heaven. The words of my spiritual mother, Mother Teresa, rang in my ears: "Death is nothing except going back to God, where He is and where we belong." Mother Teresa had helped me, even after her death, to endure the loss of my sister Barbara.

It was hard telling my brother Gene, who lives in Germany, about Barbara's death. As I told him over the phone I cried, "She had so much suffering in her life! She endured so much!" I needed to express my grief to my brother. Yet God kept flooding my heart with His peace. I remembered a quote from Saint Francis de Sales that Barbara absolutely loved. She had posted it on her blog some time ago, and I had spotted it earlier that day on the back cover of her book, *Upside Down and Back Again: Hope for the Caregiver.*

> Do not look forward in fear to the changes in life;
> Rather, look to them with full hope that as they arise,
>   God, whose very own you are, will lead you safely
>   through all things;
> And when you cannot stand it, God will carry you
>   in His arms.
> Do not fear what may happen tomorrow;
> The same understanding Father who cares for you today
>   will take care of you then and every day.
> He will either shield you from suffering or will give you
>   unfailing strength to bear it.
> Be at peace, and put aside all anxious thoughts and
>   imaginations.

Those powerful words spoke intensely to my heart.

My sister Barbara had nothing more to fear or to be concerned about. She had run the race here on earth. She was at rest now. And as for me—God must have been carrying me in His arms all that week when I could not "stand it". I have no doubt that He is still carrying me now. God will indeed carry us—we have to believe that He will!

I went home to Connecticut, and for at least a week after Barbara died, I smelled freshly baked banana bread as well as church incense. I had no idea where the smells came from because there wasn't any banana bread or incense around. I accepted the experience as a consolation from the Lord.

My High School Reunion

There's something very nerve-wracking about a high school reunion, and one of mine was coming up. I had attended a reunion ten years prior and another one before that. It's fascinating to see former classmates, but also a bit daunting too, as people can't help but notice how they measure up to each other. Nonetheless, I decided it would be nice to attend with my husband Dave.

The reunion was set up as a two-day event. The opener was held at a restaurant/bar and included a live band and cocktails. The second day we met at another location in the same town and enjoyed dinner and music.

The bar was packed when I arrived the first night. I had trouble identifying many of my classmates, though some were instantly recognizable. We all wore name tags complete with an embarrassing yearbook photo. It was fun remembering how we once looked in our carefree teenaged days.

I enjoyed speaking to some old friends and others I never really knew well in high school. A woman came over and greeted me. It was Betty! She was the girl who had been my friend in junior high school but decided to become a popular girl with no time for me. I was delightfully surprised that Betty was making time for me now. She told me that she had been reading about me on social media prior to the reunion and was quite amazed.

"You were so quiet in school," she said, "and look what you're doing now!"

She went on to tell me about her grown children and how one daughter who had a baby was seeking a place to worship. We chatted about our faith. Betty said she hoped her daughter was going to choose the Catholic Church since Betty was now feeling a bit drawn to it. It was a great conversation and my heart was soaring with amazement at God's work. *Life is so interesting,* I couldn't help but think. I promised Betty my prayers for her and her family.

The following day I attended the second part of the reunion. I brought some of my books in the car in case I had the opportunity to share them. I specifically autographed two for Betty, and when I saw her I handed them to her. We didn't see one another for the rest of the event, but I pray that Betty will be inspired by the books and perhaps decide to join the Church.

It was very nice to chat with many of my former classmates. With one old friend I got to talking about faith and he said, "I have blind faith in Jesus." I was happy to hear that he was so faithful and never missed Mass. He said he was happy to find a spiritual friend to talk with. When he had to leave I walked him out to the parking lot so that I could grab two books from my car and autograph them for him. He has since emailed to let me know how much he is enjoying them.

When I came back into the reunion I brought an armful of copies of my book *Mother Teresa and Me.* I thought since Mother Teresa was so beloved to so many, folks might enjoy reading the book even if they weren't religious. Before long many of my classmates surrounded me, asking if they could have a signed copy. I was delighted to give them away. When I graduated high school forty years before, I never would have imagined that I would one day be giving copies of my books to my classmates. I am still marveling at God's work.

A Very Blessed Surprise

I was invited to speak at a parish and as it happened it was the one that Matthew had planned to rob many moons ago. I accepted the invitation and spoke to the audience about some lessons of love that I had learned from Mother Teresa. The audience was very gracious. They lined up at my book table afterward to purchase books and to chat. As I was signing books, a woman came over to the side of the table and asked me if I remembered her. I thought she looked familiar, but couldn't think of her name.

"I am Diane Wirz."

"Oh! The neurologist I saw five years ago?" I had gone to Dr. Wirz for treatment of my brain injury after the car accident.

"Yes! I want you to know that your coming to see me played a big part in my conversion to Catholicism."

"Oh my goodness—that's wonderful! Now I remember that I gave you my saints' prayer book." My heart was ecstatic over God's amazing graces!

We chatted and exchanged phone numbers with the intention of getting in touch. We did so, and we continue to stay in contact. Diane would later tell me that she had been fascinated during our conversations at her office when I had attempted to explain little bits about the redemptive value of suffering. She couldn't quite grasp the meaning at that time but was very intrigued. After becoming a Catholic she learned much more about the beauty in the Cross of Christ.

God was clearly showing me a very unexpected blessing that night: the good that came out of the car accident. I had previously thought that perhaps my words to the teen driver about prayer might have positively impacted his life. I also thought that maybe it was a blessing that our car was in the intersection and was hit instead of the woman crossing the street in front of us. Our unfortunate circumstances might have saved her from serious injury or death. But now another exquisite fruit of the suffering was being made known to me—something I could never in a million years have imagined—my former doctor had been influenced by God's grace through me to enter the Church!

Reaching Out in Love

Saint Thérèse of Lisieux explained that Jesus "has no need of our works but only our love". This same God, she told us, has no need to inform us about His hunger or thirst but "did not fear to beg for a little water from the Samaritan woman. He was thirsty. But when He said, 'Give me to drink,' it was love for His poor creatures the Creator of the universe was seeking. He was thirsty for love" (*Story of a Soul*).

Blessed Mother Teresa said, "Jesus is God, therefore His love, His Thirst, is infinite. He the Creator of the universe asked for the love of His creatures. He thirsts for our love.... These words: 'I Thirst'—Do they echo in our souls?" (*I Thirst for You*).

The saints have consistently reminded us to share Christ's love with others, and as I have experienced, the most transforming encounters seem to happen at the most unexpected times and within what would seem like very ordinary situations.

Once I was invited to give a day-long retreat to the bishop of Corpus Christi and his staff and volunteers. After a full day of travel, the deacon who was in charge of the event dropped me at my hotel and informed me that he would be back to get me at 7:00 A.M.

I have to be honest—that night seemed like a night straight from hell. There was a very noisy bar next door, and I called the hotel's main desk a few times to ask if anything could be done about the yelling and the other commotion. Also my room was freezing cold. I had earlier asked for help with the thermostat and trusted that it would begin to work better, but no matter what I did with the thermostat my room wouldn't warm up. There was not an extra blanket to be found. The thin bedspread and sheet would have to do. My feet kept cramping up painfully, and I shivered as I prayed the night away. When the bar closed for the night there were doors slamming and the sounds of vomiting nearby. I felt annoyed, but then stopped myself mid-thought to pray for whoever it was who was sick.

At one point I looked at the clock and realized it was four o'clock. I hadn't slept yet, and I needed to be up at 5:30 A.M. *How will I ever manage to present a full retreat day?* It seemed impossible. I continued to pray. *Please, Lord, help me. You know I have to speak at the event. How can I do that with no sleep? I offer this all to You and pray for Your holy will to be accomplished.* I finally got a little less than an hour of sleep before I had to get ready for the big event. Hoping a warm shower would do me some good, I was again disappointed—the shower did not work properly and there was no shower curtain. Perhaps a little caffeine would help. Nope, I couldn't find a caffeinated tea bag. It's usually the other way around. I typically can't find a *decaffeinated* one when I need it. Maybe a little breakfast would perk me up? Well, the refried beans and tortillas were not exactly what I had in mind.

Finally, grabbing a package of dry oatmeal from the breakfast bar and hoping for some boiling water, I headed back to my room. I sat down on the chair to scarf down my modest breakfast and discovered a fairly large-sized object behind me. As it turned out I just missed sitting on a knife! This was not a mere kitchen knife. It appeared to be a weapon.

Instantly, I realized that all along I had been engaged in spiritual battle. I prayed that everything would give glory to God and decided to trust in His plan.

I texted the deacon who replied that he would soon be there to pick me up. "Please be forewarned," I wrote back, "not much sleep last night. Really need prayers." Then I texted a picture of the knife and asked, "Should I hand this in to the desk clerk?" He replied that he would be praying and that I should probably turn in the knife.

Upon getting into the kind deacon's car, I spilled out the details to him; blow by blow I told him about what had happened the night before. He said, "Do you think you can come down here to the "Body of Christ" to present an important message to this whole diocese and *not* be attacked by the evil one? We will not let him rob us of our joy!" I wholeheartedly agreed with him and asked that he would remember me in prayer throughout the day. Unless God was going to hold me up, I didn't know how I could physically stand at the podium and think straight to present all day long. I was feeling totally zapped of any energy, and knew I had to depend fully on God's grace. It seems that God often allows me to be thrust into a myriad of interesting and seemingly impossible situations so that I will fully surrender to His grace and His plan—not mine.

God never ceases to amaze me. The event went extremely well— better than I could possibly have imagined. The attendees were very touched and told me so. The kind bishop gave me generous compliments, which he also stated in a letter later on. God keeps His promises. He holds us up, especially when we are feeling weak and inadequate. His power is made perfect in weakness.

As much as I was thankful for God's amazing grace at the retreat day, I am giving thanks to Him for something even more extraordinary that happened the next morning at breakfast with some friends.

When our twenty-something waiter came to our table I noticed a very prominent slash going straight across one of his cheeks. It immediately brought to mind the knife I found in my hotel room. I also noticed that he was wearing a light blue long sleeve on one arm but not on the other and that he sported many tattoos. Each time he came to our table that distinctive scar drew my attention. After our meal, we asked our waiter if he would be so kind as to snap our photo with our cell phones. When we stopped at the register, we asked again. The lighting was a bit better in that area. The man didn't seem to mind that we asked again and was very accommodating.

Suddenly, I felt compelled to give him a blessed Miraculous Medal. Even though he was being summoned to serve another meal, I excitedly said, "Oh, just a moment please! I want to give you something." Then I hurriedly dug into my purse and took out a blessed medal. I kissed it and touched it to the medal I was wearing, the one Mother Teresa had given me. Looking into the young man's eyes I said, "I want to give you this Miraculous Medal. Here is Mary, your Mother!" I placed the medal in his outstretched hand and added, "*She* will take care of you!"

Instantly, the young man threw himself at me in a hug, his arms wrapping totally around me. He was like a little boy hugging his mother. I really think that he felt a sudden relief, that Mother Mary came straight to him through her blessed medal and was going to help him. No further words were needed. We held one another tight for a moment right there in the foyer of the family restaurant. Tears were streaming down his face. Before parting, I handed him my business card in case he ever wanted to get in touch.

After bidding good-bye to the waiter, I walked out of the restaurant with my two friends, feeling entirely speechless about what I felt Jesus and His dear Mother Mary had just accomplished. Profoundly moved, right to the core, I whispered to my friends, "I just hugged Jesus!"

One friend quickly chimed in, "He was crying!"

Then it suddenly hit me—it was *Jesus* who hugged me. I had no doubt whatsoever that that man was "Jesus in the distressing disguise of the poorest of the poor".

A couple of days later while still in Texas, I shared what had happened with another friend. She told me that the young man was most likely part of a murderous gang. *What?* Elizabeth was from Los Angeles where some of the gangs now in Corpus Christi had originated. She knew about the kind of sleeve the young man was wearing, the tattoos, and the knife slit on his face.

We never know what kind of effect we will have on someone's heart by reaching out with Christ's love. That young man seemed desperately to need a mother's hug. He responded immediately to Mother Mary in the Miraculous Medal, a sacramental of our Church. I pray that his life will be changed forever. I have kept him in my prayers and consider him to be a spiritual son.

Mother Teresa emphasized a one-on-one approach with people in need. She met each person as if he was Jesus. In his praise of Mother Teresa on the occasion of her death, Pope John Paul II described her fundamental source and inspiration:

> Her mission began every day, before dawn, in the presence of the Eucharist. In the silence of contemplation, Mother Teresa of Calcutta heard the echo of Jesus' cry on the Cross: 'I thirst.' This cry, received in the depths of her heart, spurred her to seek out Jesus in the poor, the abandoned, and the dying on the streets of Calcutta and to all the ends of the earth.

There can be no doubt—Jesus intensely thirsts for our love. He wants us to satisfy his thirst for love by loving Him and others in need of love. The question is: Will we choose to present Jesus with gall and vinegar as He was offered when hanging from the Cross? Or will we entrust our hearts to Him in full surrender to His holy will?

Time is often a very difficult thing with which to part. Yet, a selfless gift of our time is necessary to reach out in love to help others. This could mean stopping what we are doing in order to tend to the needs of someone, even if that means stepping out of our comfort zones. Mother Teresa often taught that real love often hurts; real love involves sacrifice. As Father Hardon wrote, "We love only to the degree that we are willing to suffer." Let's begin with the presence of the Eucharist in our lives and then seek out the abandoned, the lonely, and the suffering in our own midst. Again quoting Father Hardon, "There's work to be done!" We needn't be afraid of it, because God is waiting to work miracles. He certainly does not need us to make them happen. But, when we cooperate with Him, amazing transformations occur in others and in our own hearts.

Our Lord told us, "In the world you have tribulation; but be of good cheer, I have overcome the world" (Jn 16:33). There's no doubt that life can be strenuous. But, it is an incredible, hope-filled journey of continual conversion. As Saint John Paul II explained, "From the paradox of the Cross springs the answer to our most worrying questions. *Christ suffers for us.* He takes upon Himself the sufferings of everyone and redeems them. *Christ suffers with us,* enabling us to share our pain with Him. United to the suffering of Christ, human suffering becomes a means of salvation" (Message for the Twelfth World Day of the Sick,

February 11, 2004). By offering our pains, sorrows, difficulties, challenges, and everything to Jesus, we can ask Him to sanctify it all. If we wholeheartedly allow God to "write our lives", I believe we will possess perfect and abiding peace and joy no matter how crooked our path. Together, let us offer our lives in full surrender and pray: "Behold I come; . . . I delight to do your will, O my God; your law is within my heart" (Psalm 40:7–8).

ACKNOWLEDGMENTS

I am deeply grateful to my parents, Eugene Joseph and Alexandra Mary Cooper, for bringing me into the world and raising me in a large Catholic family. To my brothers and sisters—Alice Jean, Gene, Gary, Barbara, Tim, Michael, and David—thank you for being a part of my life.

Special thanks to those who helped to shape my life, including my dear grandmother Alexandra Theresa Karasiewicz Uzwiak, for her inexhaustible love and guidance. She has always been an example of heroic virtues in action. In fond appreciation for my godmother, Aunt Bertha Uzwiak Barosky, who continues to be a marvelous model Christian and holds a very special place in my heart. In affectionate memory of Aunt Mary Uzwiak Buckman, who lovingly welcomed my visits to her home. I also extend warm gratitude to Aunt Pat Cooper Ferraro for her steadfast wisdom and love.

My heartfelt thanks go to my husband, Dave, and my beloved children—Justin, Chaldea, Jessica, Joseph, and Mary-Catherine—for their continued love and support. I love you dearly!

My readership, viewership, and listenership and all I meet in my travels are much cherished. I pray for you every day. Thank you for being part of my incredible journey through life! May God continue to bless you abundantly. Please pray for me too.

Finally, I owe special thanks to Ignatius Press for asking me to write my story.

APPENDIX

Novena to Our Lady of Hope

I am the mother of fair love, and of fear, and of knowledge, and of holy hope. In me is all grace of the way and of the truth; in me is all hope of life and of virtue. Come to me all that desire me and be filled with my fruits (Sirach 24:24–26).†

O Blessed Virgin Mary, Mother of Grace, Hope of the world, hear us, your children, who cry to you.

Let Us Pray

O God, who by the marvelous protection of the Blessed Virgin Mary has strengthened us firmly in hope, grant we beseech You, that by persevering in prayer at her admonition, we may obtain the favors we devoutly implore. Through Christ Our Lord. Amen.

Prayer to Our Lady of Hope

O Mary, my Mother, I kneel before you with heavy heart. The burden of my sins oppresses me. The knowledge of my weakness discourages me. I am beset by fears and temptations of every sort. Yet I am so attached to the things of this world that instead of longing for heaven I am filled with dread at the thought of death.

From www.ewtn.com/Devotionals/novena/hope.htm.
† These verses of Sirach (also known as the Book of Ecclesiasticus) are taken from the Douay-Rheims translation of the Bible.

O Mother of Mercy, have pity on me in my distress. You are all-powerful with your Divine Son. He can refuse no request of your Immaculate Heart. Show yourself a true Mother to me by being my advocate before His throne. O Refuge of Sinners and Hope of the Hopeless, to whom shall I turn if not you?

Obtain for me, then, O Mother of Hope, the grace of true sorrow for my sins, the gift of perfect resignation to God's Holy Will, and the courage to take up my cross and follow Jesus. Beg of His Sacred Heart the special favor that I ask in this novena.

(Make your request.)

But above all I pray, O dearest Mother, that through your most powerful intercession my heart may be filled with Holy Hope, so that in life's darkest hour I may never fail to trust in God my Savior, but by walking in the way of His commandments I may merit to be united with Him, and with you in the eternal joys of heaven. Amen.

Mary, our Hope, have pity on us.

Hope of the Hopeless, pray for us.

(Say three Hail Marys.)

Note: Devotion to Our Lady of Hope is said to be one of the oldest Marian devotions. The first shrine bearing the title Our Lady of Hope was erected at Mezieres in the year 930. On January 17, 1871, Our Lady of Hope appeared in the French village of Pontmain. There she revealed herself as the Madonna of the Crucifix and gave the world her message of "hope through prayer and the Cross".

The basilica built at Pontmain by the Oblates of Mary Immaculate is one of the great French pilgrimage places, noted for its miracles of grace.

The Oblate Fathers introduced the devotion to America in 1952. Novena devotions are maintained at the Shrine of Our Lady of Hope, Oblate Fathers' Novitiate and Infirmary, Tewksbury, Massachusetts. (See more history at www.ewtn.com.)